CONNECTION AND DISCONNECTION IN REMOTE TEAMS

BREE CAGGIATI

PILAR ORTI

CONTENTS

INTRODUCTION - FROM PODCAST
TO BOOK

The year was 2019. Remote work was gaining momentum. Online collaboration tools were becoming more sophisticated, useful and accessible. "Digital nomads", "online freelance marketplaces" and "coworking spaces" were creeping into the conversations about "the future of work".

At the same time, podcasting was growing in popularity. And in the business field, podcasters were using the most intimate of mediums to advocate for new ways of working and to challenge current practices.

Listeners were also hungry for more podcasts to inspire them to make career changes and give them information to help them advocate for diverse collaboration styles at work.

One of us, Pilar Orti, was already speaking, advocating, and coaching organisations and teams on how to make the best out of online collaboration. She'd already published about 200 episodes of the 21st Century Work Life podcast and she found that remote work veterans, pioneers and new voices were eager to share their stories. The 21st Century Work Life podcast was a platform to speak about new breakthroughs and advocate for online methodologies that didn't require bricks and mortar to enable the best of collaborations and creations.

Acknowledging that both Pilar and her podcast collaborator Maya Middlemiss were already stretched out, she took advantage of the global reach of the show and asked for help.

"If anyone out there would like to help us put out more content, let me know."

One listener took the bait.

Tim Burgess, co-founder of Shield GEO and previous guest on the show offered his fully-distributed (100% remote) company as a partner for a new season.

What followed was a seven episode investigation into the connection levels of remote workers which we called "Connection and Disconnection in Remote Teams".

AN EMERGING CONCERN

We started the project before the Covid-19 pandemic lockdowns forced a large percentage of office workers to operate from their homes, but after remote work advocates had already been making headway on the merits of this lifestyle. The episodes streamed between February and May 2020.

At the time, the risk of loneliness was emerging as a topic of discussion within remote work circles. Some early-adopters had gathered evidence of how the work style was progressing long-term and advocates were revealing the nuances beyond the initial positives.

As Pilar put it in our opening episode[1], "We've gotten over the 'Wow, remote work is fantastic' phase, and now we're in the 'Okay, what are the long-term implications of this work style?' phase."

Around that same time, as part of its consumer research initiative, Shield GEO, had completed a research project with students from Sydney University where they aimed to identify gaps in support for remote workers. As Tim explained, "Basically, the students were looking at where people are asking questions online in various mediums that aren't really getting answered. One of the topics they came across was the loneliness and disconnection that can emerge when you're separated from your colleagues."

Bree Caggiati, a journalist at Shield GEO at the time, stepped in to host and edit the series, investigating the topic through research, interviews and round-table discussions.

We (Bree and Pilar) also had personal interests in understanding this topic further. As professionals who had experienced the ups and downs of remote work firsthand, we were living with the very challenges we were addressing in the series.

For Bree, the journey began with a move from Brisbane, Australia to Calgary, Canada. Despite initially feeling equipped for isolated work thanks to years of freelancing, she quickly discovered how different the experience was when working within a team separated not just by distance but by time zones as well. Now that the natural rhythm of spontaneous requests and email exchanges were absent throughout the day, she found herself struggling with procrastination, often working late into the night to catch up. Without her established routine in Australia, this was a cycle that was hard to break out of. This experience brought into sharp focus the realities of remote work – while it offered flexibility, it also increased the risk of disconnection.

Pilar, on the other hand, was a long-time advocate for remote work as an option comparable – and in some cases superior – to office-based schedules. As the pandemic lockdowns came to an end and people started returning to the office, it became important for her to demonstrate that while human connection can be challenging in remote work, it shouldn't be seen as a shortcoming of the medium itself. In fact, one of the reasons Pilar has embraced remote work is that it allows her to build strong relationships with people, regardless of where they are based.

These touch points became the foundations for our exploration into loneliness, isolation and disconnection among remote workers. It was a topic we quickly found expanded to workers of all kinds and eventually, society at large.

Over a series of months Bree interviewed psychologists, researchers, remote work advocates, HR professionals and individual contributors gathering insights, anecdotes and research on the topic. It was through these conversations that we first discovered how expansive this issue really is. We saw how our individual experiences, while unique, echoed broader trends in the remote work landscape. We recognised that by sharing our stories and insights, we could contribute to a larger conversation about making remote work not just feasible, but truly fulfilling.

Throughout the season we noticed several themes emerge, including the prevalence of isolation and disconnection, the shared responsibility for connection in organisations, the importance of self-reflection, and the need for ongoing conversations and support.

The episodes were produced and released in real time, initially with the aim to encourage audience input and collaboration along the way. However, the release timeframe gave us the opportunity to address what was happening as the world plunged into lockdowns in response to the Covid-19 pandemic in March 2020.

As our audience expanded exponentially, it became even more clear to us how nuanced this topic really was. Our work experiences could not be separated from our personal lives, no matter where that work happened.

By the time we finished the series in May 2020, the future of remote work and its implications for society was largely still unclear. Would the pandemic give way to lasting flexibility for all office workers? Should businesses expand their search beyond their city limits when finding new talent? Given how quickly new ways of working were being adopted, would organisations take the time to implement strategies that supported remote work, or would they continue with their impromptu arrangements and risk encountering problems later?

EVOLVING THE CONVERSATION

The podcast season was intended to start a dialogue and encourage further reflection and action on the issue for both employers and employees. We hoped it would encourage more openness in the workplace about discussing the contexts of employees' lives as well as their emotional health.

In our concluding episode[2], our collaborator and show notes writer, Maya Middlemiss, summed this sentiment up well by saying:

"I hope this will form part of an ongoing conversation in every workplace where we can be just a little bit more open to talking about our contexts, our emotional health, our needs generally. Whether that's in the context of loneliness and isolation, or things like stress or other kinds of mental health problems which we spent decades in the workplace pretending didn't exist, or was all the individual's problem. Now we're starting to have a more sophisticated way of looking at that in society in general and in work, too."

For us, putting the season together introduced us to new perspectives. Our initial concept had evolved from an attempt to support a small group – lonely remote workers – into a comprehensive exploration of disconnection and how it can affect *everyone*. We now understood some of its causes, its impacts, and provided some suggested solutions across all levels of an organisation, focusing primarily on practices such as self-reflection, empathy and periodic check-ins to cater to evolving needs rather than prescriptive ideas like one-off team building activities or enforcing camera-on meetings.

While we acknowledged the immediate relevance of the topic during the pandemic, we recognised there would be an ongoing need into the future to address issues of disconnection and emotional wellbeing in the workplace – and that the conversation should continue.

Today, five years later, knowledge-based workplaces exist across the full spectrum – often hybrid, often flexible, sometimes remote or purely in-office – but due to the nature of the introduction to these models, they are also often disorganised or operating without the proper infrastructure to thrive.

More recently, hybrid or remote offices are opting to mandate in-office attendance, but at the same time our Western society is reportedly lonelier than ever.

Technology has evolved in ways we didn't expect, and new platforms have established themselves as the default collaboration tools for many organisations. (For example, you will notice ample reference to Slack in the text, as it was the most ubiquitous chat-based collaboration tool at the time of recording the season. However, there are no references to MSTeams, which grew in popularity during the pandemic.)

From a personal perspective, Pilar is now an author and qualified Pilates teacher and Bree is writing for magazines in a different industry – but the project and the topic remain close to our hearts.

In 2024 we revisited Connection and Disconnection in Remote Teams with fresh eyes and came to the conclusion that the information was as pertinent as ever. With the knowledge we've gained since then, it felt like the perfect time to continue the conversation.

Furthermore, in revisiting this material, we've also benefited from the perspectives of our first-draft readers who brought additional insights to the topic. Their varied professional backgrounds helped us refine our thinking and expand our analysis. We've addressed their feedback by clarifying and expanding on certain concepts, and even included some of their own insights.

This collaborative approach reflects our belief that understanding workplace connection requires diverse viewpoints and that the conversation around the different aspects of remote work continues to evolve.

WHAT WE OFFER YOU

The text you're about to read (or the words you're hearing if you're listening to the audiobook) is an extension of our initial podcast season. We've kept an informal tone, touching on our personal experiences, bringing in different voices to add different perspectives and adding studies and examples from sources beyond our initial research.

Our aim is to help you understand this complex issue, whether you're an employee seeking connection, a manager building team cohesion, or working towards truly supporting remote work in your organisation.

The first four chapters present the complex relationship between remote work in organisations and workplace connection:

- **Chapter 1** introduces the concept of connection and disconnection in remote teams, highlighting the shift in remote work dynamics since the start of the Covid-19 pandemic.
- **Chapter 2** focuses on why connection is important, explaining that loneliness, physical isolation and disconnection from a workplace's culture, workflow, and information can all have detrimental effects on an individual, their team, and the broader company.
- **Chapter 3** examines the effect of "remote" on loneliness, and we suggest that the context in which remote work takes place matters more than whether someone works remotely or not.
- In **Chapter 4** we ask (and attempt to answer) the question: Who is responsible for preventing disconnection and loneliness in organisations?

For the second part of the book, we have collected practical advice from our guests and other sources.

- **Chapter 5** encompasses the broader, organisation-wide initiatives that create the framework for connection.
- **Chapters 6 and** 7 focus on managerial support: how managers (and other team members) can open up the conversation around loneliness, how teamwork can be structured to enable connection, and how managers can support individuals.
- **Chapter 8** is full of individual strategies anyone can implement, even if their work environment is less than ideal.
- In **Chapter 9**, we take out our crystal ball and hypothesise how technology might bring collaborators both together and apart.
- Finally, **Chapter 10** lays down five steps for sustainable connection and acknowledges the importance of relationship management in preventing loneliness.

The chapters are followed by a short summary and a collection of questions that you can reflect on yourself, or better still, with your team.

As in the podcast season that preceded this book, we have chosen not to address this topic in a prescriptive manner. The experience of connection or disconnection in remote work is highly individual. However, it's worth mentioning that our perspective is limited. While we've aimed to approach this from various angles, we're aware that there are some stones left unturned.

As such, we invite you, the reader, to engage actively with the content. Reflect on your own experiences, challenge our ideas, and consider how the concepts we discuss apply to your unique situation.

We'll provide practical tips and strategies, but we also encourage you to approach them with a spirit of experimentation. What works for one person or team may not work for another, and the landscape of remote work is continually evolving.

OUR CAST OF CHARACTERS (A TO Z)

To give colour and context to these chapters we have included some quotes and stories from our podcast guests, as well as updated musings from our own lives.

Tim Burgess

Tim is the co-founder of Contractor Taxation, a service connecting contractors with umbrella companies supporting them to remain compliant through international contracts, and the former co-founder of employer of record Shield GEO.
Tim shares stories from early in his career as a remote worker without support as well as his experience developing and leading a team of 70 people across 17 countries.

Isabel Collins

Isabel is a consultant and founder of Belonging Space, providing diagnosis, coaching and practical solutions for clients to nurture belonging.
Isabel shares what it means to feel a sense of belonging and what organisations and managers can do to facilitate this.

Teresa Douglas

Teresa is a seasoned project manager and programme driver who has managed a number of high-performance remote and hybrid teams to achieve their goals.

Teresa shares some of her own experiences managing remote teams as well as some anecdotal evidence from some personal research.

Laurel Farrer

Laurel is an internationally-renowned thought leader on the topic of remote work and virtual organisational development. She is the founder of Distribute, a consulting firm specialising exclusively in remote work and virtual organisational development. Laurel shares her expertise on these topics.

Dr. Julianne Holt-Lunstad

Dr. Holt-Lunstad is a professor of psychology and neuroscience and director of the Social Connection & Health Lab at Brigham Young University. She is also the founding scientific chair and board member for the US Foundation for Social Connection and the Global Initiative on Loneliness and Connection.
Dr. Holt-Lunstad shares findings from her seminal research on the effects of loneliness on our physical health as well as some hypotheses on why we feel lonely at all.

Asia Hundley

Asia is an account manager for Spanish manufacturing company CUBPRO.
At the time of recording, Asia was a remote worker from the US living and working in Spain. She shares her personal experiences of feeling disconnected and lonely and what helped.

Dr. Richard MacKinnon

Dr. MacKinnon is a chartered coaching psychologist, chartered occupational psychologist and the founder of WorkLifePsych, a team of accredited and experienced workplace psychologists providing coaching, development programmes and training.

Dr. MacKinnon shares some common themes that occur for struggling workplaces and individuals as well as some solutions that have worked for his clients.

Maya Middlemiss

Maya has been working remotely for over 25 years and is the founder of Remote Work Europe, where she supports individuals working remotely, and consults and speaks for teams and organisations. At the time of recording the Connection and Disconnection season, she was an associate at Virtual not Distant, where she created content and co-hosted the "What's Going On" segments on the 21st Century Work Life podcast.

Brian Rhea

Brian is the head of product at After.com, a company redefining the end-of-life planning process. At the time of the podcast season, Brian was developing a culture tool to help teams determine how connected their teams felt day-to-day. He shares the ideation process and some of his own experiences that led to pursuing this.

Courtney Seiter

Courtney is the people partner at The Browser Company and former director of people at Buffer. She shares some of Buffer's programmes and tools that help its remote team remain connected.

Tara Vasdani

Tara is the managing partner and founder of Remote Law Canada, a law firm specialising in civil litigation, employment law, real estate and remote work. She shares her expertise on the topic of duty of care as it pertains to remote employers and their employees.

Marcus Wermuth

Marcus is the vice president of engineering at Safety Cybersecurity and a former senior engineering manager at Buffer. He shares his experience as a manager of remote teams and some solutions to common problems in the workplace.

Our First-Draft Readers

As part of our writing process, we sought feedback from a few trusted friends and family members to share their thoughts and reactions to the text. They often provided us with new perspectives, which we have incorporated throughout the book.

And finally...

You, the reader.

We'd like to encourage you to read through our examples, advice and experiences and reflect on to what extent they apply to you and your situation.

Our hope is that this book will serve as a resource as you build out the practices that serve you best.

Whether you're a team leader looking to strengthen your distributed team, an individual trying to navigate the complexities of remote work, or an organisation aiming to build a connected remote culture, we hope this book sparks conversations that will prevent loneliness from standing in the way of people fully enjoying remote work.

Bree Caggiati and Pilar Orti
Melbourne / London 2025

DEFINING THE ISSUE

A s it stands, with the advancement of technology, high speed internet and continually evolving online communities and platforms, our world seems more connected than ever.

The explosion of remote work for knowledge workers during the Covid-19 pandemic in 2020 led to widespread embrace of online tools including video calls that is still prevalent today, even among hybrid or office-first workplaces.

Despite this, Western society has found itself experiencing unprecedented levels of loneliness and social isolation.

But what exactly do we mean when we talk about loneliness and social isolation? And how, if at all, are they related to disconnection?

THE CONNECTION CONUNDRUM

Though often used interchangeably, the terms loneliness and social isolation describe distinct experiences.

Dr. Julianne Holt-Lunstad, a professor of psychology and neuroscience and director of the Social Connection & Health Lab at Brigham Young University, puts it this way:

"Social isolation refers to objectively being alone, having few relationships or infrequent social contacts; whereas loneliness refers to subjectively feeling alone, or the discrepancy between one's desired level of connection and one's actual level."

Others have taken this idea further to suggest that while social isolation can contribute to feelings of loneliness, it isn't the only cause. Nor is it essential to feeling lonely.

As Suzanne Degges-White wrote in a Psychology Today article, "the presence of loneliness reflects the absence of connection, not the absence of people".

This is why we are particularly focused on *connection and disconnection* in this book.

As long term remote workers, and as co-authors who have never physically met, we know we can feel deeply connected to people on the other side of the world. We also know that being physically near someone doesn't guarantee feeling connected – particularly in a work setting.

It's this "connection conundrum" that we're interested in exploring.

Despite its many benefits, the very technology that enables us to work from anywhere can also contribute to us feeling isolated and disconnected from our work and our teams.

Connection is more than just having a stable internet connection or being reachable via instant messaging. True connection in a work setting (remote or otherwise) encompasses a sense of belonging, shared purpose, and meaningful engagement with colleagues and the work itself. It's about feeling part of a team or organisation even when you're physically apart from your colleagues.

Disconnection, on the other hand, can manifest in unexpected ways.

While Dr. Holt-Lunstad and Suzanne Degges-White describe loneliness as the absence of connection, disconnection doesn't always have to carry the emotional weight of loneliness.

Sometimes, it's a subtle feeling of being out of sync with your team or a creeping sense of professional stagnation. For some, disconnection might mean struggling to build trust with colleagues they've never met in person. For others, it could be the challenge of staying motivated without the energy of a shared workspace.

But it's when these moments of disconnection, which are normal and common, go unchecked that they can compound into a more chronic state of loneliness, which is something that can have significant impacts (more on this in Chapter 2).

Tech separates us

Tech brings us together

The connection conundrum

Of course, feelings of disconnection aren't unique to remote work. Even in traditional office settings, employees can (and often do) feel disconnected from their colleagues or their work. However, remote work has the potential to amplify these challenges and introduce new dimensions to them.

Despite some return-to-office initiatives, remote work is more common than ever. Professionals across industries often find themselves collaborating with colleagues they may never meet in person, managing teams across time zones, and navigating the blurred lines between home and office. This shift brings with it unprecedented flexibility and opportunity, but also introduces a new set of challenges – challenges that strike at the very heart of how we connect as human beings in a professional context.

WHY THIS MATTERS

The connection conundrum isn't just an interesting philosophical question – it has real, tangible impacts on individuals, teams, and organisations.

On an individual level, the quality of connection we experience in our work directly affects our wellbeing and job satisfaction. When we feel connected to our colleagues and our work, we're more likely to be engaged, motivated, and fulfilled. This sense of connection is what protects us against the potential isolation of remote work, supporting our mental health and overall life satisfaction.

Conversely, persistent feelings of disconnection can lead to a host of problems. Remote workers might experience decreased motivation, increased stress, and even burnout. The lack of clear boundaries between work and personal life can lead to overwork or difficulty in "switching off," impacting both productivity and personal relationships.

From an organisational perspective, the stakes are equally high. Companies that successfully foster connection in their remote teams often see benefits in productivity, creativity, and employee retention. A connected team is more likely to collaborate effectively, share knowledge freely, and remain loyal to the organisation.

On the other hand, disconnection can lead to communication

breakdowns, misaligned goals, and a fragmented company culture. It can make it challenging to build trust and rapport among team members, potentially impacting the quality of work and the ability to innovate. Moreover, feelings of disconnection can even be the cause of individuals leaving certain teams and companies.

The implications extend beyond individual companies to the broader economy and society. While many of us understand the emotional impacts of these experiences, evidence is increasingly indicating they also impact our health and economies.[1]

Dr Holt-Lunstad's research (which we will come back to more thoroughly in the next chapter) has found that chronic loneliness and social isolation can be as damaging to our health as smoking 15 cigarettes a day. It increases our risk of heart disease, stroke, and premature death and can affect our immune systems, our sleeping patterns, and even how our genes express themselves. The economic costs are equally staggering, with billions spent annually on related healthcare expenses and lost productivity.

HOPE ISN'T LOST

Despite these sobering realities, we strongly believe there's reason for hope. Understanding loneliness and social isolation – their causes, effects, and potential solutions – is the first step toward addressing this crisis.

As we'll explore throughout this book, human beings are remarkably resilient and adaptable. We have an innate capacity for connection that, when properly supported and nurtured, can help us build bridges across the divides that separate us.

As remote work becomes a more permanent fixture in our professional landscape, our ability to make it sustainable and fulfilling will shape the future of work itself. Will remote work lead to a more balanced, satisfying professional life? Or will it exacerbate issues of isolation and burnout? The answers to these questions depend largely on how we address the challenge of connection.

Furthermore, the skills we develop in fostering connection in remote work environments have the potential to enhance our relationships and communities beyond the professional sphere. We believe learning to build meaningful connections across physical distances can enrich our personal lives and contribute to a more connected society as a whole.

SUMMARY

- Social isolation is defined as objectively being alone with few relationships or infrequent social contacts, while loneliness refers to the subjective feeling of being alone or the discrepancy between one's desired and actual level of connection.

- The ability to foster connection in remote work can lead to a more balanced and satisfying professional life and can also enhance relationships and communities outside of work.

- The exploration of connection and disconnection in remote teams is a personal journey, acknowledging the challenges and opportunities of remote work.

- There is no one-size-fits-all solution to fostering connection in remote teams; a nuanced approach is needed to acknowledge diverse needs and preferences.

CONTINUING THE CONVERSATION - QUESTIONS FOR YOU AND YOUR TEAM

1. What does connection to the work itself, to our colleagues, and to the company as a whole currently look like for us in our specific work context?

2. How has our team's understanding of connection evolved since the shift to more remote or hybrid work models?

3. What are the potential long-term implications of remote work on our team's dynamics and overall wellbeing?

4. How can we move beyond the initial excitement of remote work to address the more nuanced challenges of maintaining connection and addressing isolation?

2

THE COST OF DISCONNECTION

There is something fundamental to us about connection. Inherently, it's something most of us want and subconsciously seek out.

In fact, as Dr. Julianne Holt-Lunstad shared with us in episode three, there is research[1] that suggests loneliness functions similarly to other basic human needs.

"This really stems from the idea that humans are social creatures, and much like other kinds of social animals, we thrive in groups. Being part of a group is adaptive for survival...not only from a safety standpoint, but also pooling of resources, [it] not only helps us manage risk, but also manage effort," she explained. "It's argued that loneliness is a biological drive much like hunger or thirst – hunger motivates us to seek out food, thirst motivates us to seek out water and loneliness motivates us to seek out relationships."

While each of these states of being are somewhat unpleasant, they serve a purpose pushing us towards something ultimately more beneficial than the initial discomfort.

However, there are various factors, including how our environments are structured, that can disrupt or interfere with these motivations. Just as the creation of highly-processed foods has meant we may seek out lower-nutritional options when we are hungry due to their convenience, we may also be more prone to seek out lower-impact connection points, despite the lessened benefits. For example, writing a quick chat message asking, "How was your day?" as we wait for the bus takes much less time and energy than picking up the phone to have a good chat.

Dr. Holt-Lunstad also compares loneliness to feelings of pain.

"Physical pain is this unpleasant state but is highly motivating. If we had our hand on a hot stove, it's that pain that motivates us to remove it to prevent tissue damage, and so, even though no one likes to experience pain – pain is awful – it nonetheless is incredibly important for survival," she said. "What this suggests is that loneliness may be adaptive in the long run. Ultimately, we don't want to eliminate loneliness altogether. Because it is this important signal to us. But it's when it becomes something that we experience chronically that it can become maladaptive."[2]

It's the long term impacts of chronic loneliness that make catching disconnection early on so important.

THE LONELINESS EPIDEMIC

As of April 2025, several countries have implemented national strategies to address loneliness, recognising it as a significant public health concern.

The United Kingdom pioneered this effort in 2018 by appointing a Minister for Loneliness[3] and launching "A Connected Society" strategy[4], which includes initiatives like social prescribing (non-medical support linking patients to community resources) and workplace pledges. Japan followed suit in 2021, establishing a similar ministerial role to combat social isolation, particularly among its hikikomori population, which describes socially withdrawn individuals avoiding outside interaction[5].

Denmark introduced its first national strategy in 2023[6], aiming to halve loneliness by 2040 through collaboration across sectors such as education, employment, and healthcare. Australia has developed multiple national documents addressing loneliness, including a 2021 strategy produced by Ending Loneliness Together in partnership with R U OK? and the Australian Psychological Society[7]. The Netherlands launched the "One Against Loneliness" action programme (2022–2025)[8], focusing on community engagement and support for vulnerable groups. Ireland's Health Service Executive introduced the "Stronger Together" mental health promotion plan (2022–2027)[9], which includes measures to address loneliness and social isolation.

South Korea implemented a programme providing monthly stipends to socially isolated youth aged 9–24[10], encouraging them to re-engage with society through education and employment opportunities. While the United States lacks a formal national loneliness strategy, the Surgeon General issued an advisory in 2023[11] highlighting loneliness as a public health crisis.

The vast amount of programmes and initiatives available reflect the growing global recognition of loneliness as a problem of concern, one that requires a coordinated policy response.

This increased awareness of loneliness and social isolation has led to a surge in research, some of which we will share here. However, it's worth noting that while many of its impacts are now well documented, the long-term consequences of loneliness are still being studied.

WORKPLACE IMPACTS

Loneliness, physical isolation and disconnection from a workplace's culture, workflow and information can all have detrimental effects on an individual, their team and the broader company.

Fragmented communication and documentation

When individuals don't have access to all the information they need to complete their tasks, it can slow down workflow and lead to frustration, loss of trust within teams or misaligned resources. This often happens when there is no centralised location to store company information and documentation, or a lack of a structured workflow program or online noticeboard. In these cases, one person or team is likely the gatekeeper of certain workplace knowledge, which may work while an organisation is small but quickly becomes unmanageable as soon as that person is busy, away from their desk or moves on from the company.

Early on in her career, Bree worked for a team without a centralised storage process. Most of the information was shared through meetings or emails and was often siloed to individual people. For the most part this worked perfectly fine. Whenever a new task came up there was someone to answer questions and Bree was always taking personal notes to revisit later. However, at one point, her manager went on holiday without leaving a detailed handover document behind. The flaws of this system became immediately obvious.

In one case, Bree was asked to take on a task her manager was usually in charge of and no one else in the team knew how to complete. What followed was hours of troubleshooting, searching through emails and messages for any information previously shared, reaching out to other team members in other locations, looking for answers on Google and eventually having to wait until her manager returned to learn the process before proceeding.

While pushing back the deadline didn't impact the company too significantly, the experience did affect Bree's stress levels and contributed to some feelings of isolation. It took away time from her other tasks and eroded some trust with her manager – something that could have been avoided had there been a documented process stored in a centralised location.

Although this example could occur in any workplace, it's particularly common in hybrid setups where organisations haven't invested in creating the appropriate infrastructure to support work in multiple locations. According to internationally renowned remote work expert Laurel Farrer, who has 20 years' experience helping organisations build effective distributed teams, many organisations mistakenly believe that simply allowing employees to work from home constitutes effective remote work.

"Most people are going into this change (transitioning from the office to remote) completely organically and incorrectly assuming that just sending somebody away from the office makes them a remote worker," she says in episode four[12]. "That's exactly why we see that informational isolation, that social isolation. That's why we also see discrimination (based on worker location) – because they're not intentionally making this change and building the infrastructure to support it."

Misaligned vision

This kind of disconnection can also extend beyond the daily work requirements of process documentation and task-specific information and result in individuals or entire teams feeling alienated from the high-level vision, values or trajectory of the company. This can occur for a number of reasons including mergers or acquisitions, a shift in top level strategy, a misaligned hire or a lack of communication between C-suite and the rest of the company.

When this disconnect occurs it can cause a number of issues within an organisation. For example, without proper understanding of the company goals and ambitions it can be easy for teams or individuals to misuse budget and resources as they attempt to follow an old or incorrect direction.

These scenarios can also affect the mood and culture of the company. If the leadership acts in ways that are unexpected or different to what they had previously described, it can erode trust with the rest of the team. Without trust, individuals and teams are more likely to disengage from the work, reducing their efforts and long-term commitment to the company.

Tim Burgess is a reflective and experienced leader who has spent years thinking about how to build and support remote teams, especially during his time as co-founder of the fully distributed company Shield GEO. He was the one who first suggested loneliness as a theme for our podcast season. Tim suggests that disconnected individuals are also less likely to be open to change or forgiving of any bumps in the road that may occur throughout their time with a company. He nailed it in episode three[13] when he said: "If you're disengaged, you're like, 'Final straw. That's it. I'm out of here'".

In contrast, an individual that has felt connected to their team and company would be less affected by shifts in strategy or direction because they have more evidence of the company being open with them.

Interpersonal issues

When we feel lonely it often affects our mood and self-esteem in the workplace and beyond. This could mean we are less likely to contribute in meetings or be open to collaboration. Not only does this reduce the ideas and information available to a team, it can also disrupt team dynamics, expanding the disconnection experience.

As a workplace psychologist, Dr. Richard MacKinnon has observed that disconnection often underlies many common workplace issues. Through his extensive work with individuals facing workplace challenges, in addition to the existing scientific research, he has found that humans have a fundamental need for connection – one that, when unfulfilled, can trigger a cascade of negative effects. "When people feel disconnected, their mood and self-perception suffer, often leading to self-doubt and disengagement," he said. "This withdrawal typically manifests as reduced effort and commitment to their work. People might justify pulling back by questioning why they should invest in an environment where they don't feel supported. For many, this downward spiral of disconnection and disengagement ultimately ends in their departure from the organisation."

The downward spiral of disconnection

Home life impacts

When we work remotely, oftentimes that means working from our homes. This can mean separate office spaces, but it can also mean kitchen tables, couches and bedrooms. When we think of the effects of a person feeling isolated and disconnected from work, for remote workers it's likely this will impact the people they live with too.

As Tim explains, "Because there's less of a buffer between your work experience and your home experience in remote work, it might be harder to make that transition (from work life to home life). You might carry more of your work experience into your home experience, especially if you're a bit isolated."

When you're disconnected from your team or manager you might feel frustration with them around certain tasks or interactions. As we saw in Bree's earlier example, teams that don't use central or visible workflow systems often experience frustration around document sharing and version history. Managers may ask individuals to resend documents they can't find or even reassign tasks that are already completed simply because the workflow isn't easily visible. When behaviours like these (and others) are repeated, it can erode trust and motivation within the team.

When these frustrations and resentments pile up, the emotional implications can affect the home life of remote workers. Without the distance and processing time between a potential incident and home life via time in the office and the subsequent commute, remote workers may find themselves immediately venting to a partner or family member or letting their bad mood get the better of them given they are working in the comfort of their own home.

HEALTH IMPLICATIONS

While our focus for this book is the workplace, we know that loneliness and social isolation have much broader impacts on our lives.

In 2010, as part of her ongoing research into loneliness, Dr. Holt-Lunstaad led a meta-analysis study[14] to determine whether our social relationships can affect our risk for mortality.

The seminal work analysed 148 studies (308,849 participants) to find that strong social relationships increased odds of survival by 50%. This is as beneficial as quitting smoking, more impactful than well-known risk factors like obesity and physical inactivity and at a similar magnitude to other major health interventions.

When we recorded the Connection and Disconnection in Remote Teams season Dr. Holt-Lunstad spoke to us about her work, and provided some context for the importance of addressing loneliness and social isolation, not just in the workplace, but on a societal level.

"I think people recognise that our relationships might influence our emotional wellbeing, how happy or satisfied we feel. But most people don't recognise the powerful effects that it has on our actual physical health," she said.

What Julianne found was that regardless of whether someone was healthy or ill, people who are more socially connected lived longer.

The study showed quantity and quality of relationships mattered when considering the impact on mortality, with complex measures of social integration showing the strongest effect (91% increased odds of survival). In contrast, simple binary measures (like living alone vs. not) showed the weakest effect.

It's important to note here that the health effects of loneliness and social isolation are not reduced to diseases and concerns that develop later in life. According to Julianne, we're seeing health effects among younger populations as well, including increases in hypertension or inflammatory markers.

In fact, a 2025 study published in Nature Human Behaviour[15] found higher levels of specific proteins in people who reported social isolation or loneliness. Researchers analysed data from over 42,000 participants from the UK Biobank project. These individuals were followed for nearly 14 years, providing an unprecedented look at how social connection – or lack thereof – affects our physical health. Within this group, approximately 9.3% reported experiencing social isolation, while 6.4% reported feelings of loneliness. These individuals showed distinctly different protein profiles in their blood compared to their more connected peers.

The study identified 175 proteins associated with social isolation and 26 proteins linked to loneliness, with many overlapping between the two conditions. These proteins played important roles in inflammation, immune system function and antiviral responses. Furthermore, 90% of the identified proteins were linked to mortality risk, with roughly half associated with cardiovascular disease, type 2 diabetes and stroke. One protein, known as ADM, proved particularly significant, explaining approximately 7.5% of the connection between loneliness and various disease risks.

Professor Barbara Sahakian from the University of Cambridge, a co-author of the study, told *The Guardian*[16] that these findings should prompt a fundamental shift in how we view social connection.

"We've got to start to get people to realise that it's part of a health thing, both for their mental health and their wellbeing but also for their physical health, that they have to remain connected with other people," she said.

ECONOMIC CONSEQUENCES

With health impacts of this magnitude, we're naturally seeing some economic ones follow.

Lidia Engel and Cathrine Mihalopoulos shared in their article for the *Medical Journal Australia*[17] that the total cost of loneliness in Australia was estimated around AU$2.7 billion (or AU$1565 for each person who becomes or remains lonely).

They said adults aged 55 years or older accounted for more than a third of the costs and that the costs were mainly associated with increases in health service use, sick leave and lifestyle behaviour. While older adults do have an increase in chronic conditions, Engel and Mihalopoulos also cited studies that found lonely adults could be using health service visits to meet their need for interaction and interpersonal stimulation.

There are costs in a workplace context too. Health insurer Cigna found that loneliness has cost employers approximately US$154 billion annually.[18]

"Lonely workers had significantly higher rates of stress-related absenteeism," Anne Bowers, a senior health services researcher with Cigna told the publication. "They missed more than five additional work days per year than workers who are not lonely. They were twice as likely to report intention of quitting their jobs in the next twelve months."

This lack of productivity and employee turnover was said to be the cause of the increase to employer costs.

Having explored the broader economic, health, and organisational impacts of loneliness at work, we now turn to the context at the heart of this book – remote teams – where these challenges can take on a distinct shape. In the next chapter, we look at how the experience of loneliness is shaped by the conditions of remote work – and why that context matters.

SUMMARY

- Disconnection affects multiple aspects of life, including the workplace, home life, and our health.

- In the workplace, issues like information isolation and a misaligned vision between teams or leadership can erode trust and contribute to disconnection.

- Working from home can mean work-related frustrations can directly impact family relationships.

- Research shows that socially connected people live longer.

- Loneliness has economic consequences in the overuse of medical resources and workers taking more sick days.

CONTINUING THE CONVERSATION

1. How might information isolation be manifested within our team, and what steps can we take to improve information flow and accessibility?

2. In what ways can disconnection from our workplace's culture affect individual team members, and what can we do to foster a stronger sense of belonging?

3. Have we observed any instances where loneliness or disconnection has led to decreased productivity or increased absenteeism within our team? How can we address these issues proactively?

4. How do our team's current practices and systems support or hinder the development of trust among team members?

3

THE EFFECT OF "REMOTE" ON LONELINESS

When we talk about loneliness in remote teams, it's tempting to draw a direct line between working away from others and feeling isolated. The logic seems straightforward: remote work equals being physically separate from colleagues, therefore remote workers must experience more loneliness. But, loneliness at work isn't unique to remote teams – it's a pervasive challenge across all work environments and society at large. In this chapter, we examine the unique challenges that remote work brings while debunking common myths about loneliness in distributed teams.

THE BIGGER PICTURE

According to Gallup's State of the Global Workplace 2024 report, one in five employees worldwide reported feeling lonely at work. This statistic spans all work environments – from office-based organisations to hybrid arrangements and fully remote setups. Loneliness doesn't discriminate based on work location.[1]

Cultural, economic, demographic, and technological factors all play roles in how people experience loneliness, many of which have nothing to do with where someone performs their work. An employee can feel profoundly disconnected while sitting in a crowded office, just as a remote worker might feel deeply connected to their team despite physical distance.

As we've already seen, work represents a significant part of our lives and social connections and so it's important to acknowledge that loneliness at work can have an impact on our lives as a whole. Attributing these feelings solely to remote work oversimplifies a complex issue and potentially misdirects efforts to address it.

When we look beyond the headlines of Gallup's report, we see a more nuanced picture. While 25% of remote workers reported experiencing loneliness "a lot of the day yesterday," the differences between remote, hybrid, and on-site workers were minimal when examined across regions.

In the US and Canada, 19% of exclusively remote workers experienced loneliness compared to 17% of hybrid workers and 18% of on-site workers. Across Latin America and the Caribbean's diverse regions, the rates remained notably consistent: 12% for remote workers, 13% for hybrid, and 13% for on-site. Europe also showed distinct patterns across its varied cultural landscape, with 22% of remote workers reporting loneliness compared to 14% of hybrid and 12% of on-site workers.

With this in mind, pure physical distance is unlikely to be causing the feelings of disconnection. In the *Harvard Business Review* article 'We're Still Lonely at Work'[2], the authors further challenge the remote work-loneliness connection. Their study found that the number of days spent in the office had no impact on reported levels of loneliness. Whether someone worked five days in the office or just two made no difference to their feelings of connection.

In fact, the study found that company-sponsored social opportunities and individual personality traits were more significant drivers of loneliness than work location. Furthermore, the same study revealed that even participants reporting high levels of loneliness conducted nearly half (47%) of their work interactions in person, suggesting that physical presence alone doesn't prevent feelings of isolation. This should be enough to remove "combating loneliness" from the list of reasons why companies insist on people using their offices.

THE LONELY OFFICE

Tim Burgess' first encounter with loneliness and disconnection happened in an office environment. In his initial job after university, Tim worked for a recruitment company in Australia. After about a year, he was asked to move to the UK, where he was transferred to a tiny, one-person office in central London. His daily interactions were limited to brief exchanges with security guards and receptionists, and the occasional conversation with clients - if he was fortunate enough to get through their voicemail. As a recruiter, he often faced the challenge of people avoiding his calls.

At 25, Tim found himself increasingly aware that something about this isolated work environment was affecting him, though he couldn't quite put his finger on what. What he didn't immediately recognise was that he was experiencing loneliness. Despite living in a shared house and having an active social life, the isolation of his workdays made it hard to stay motivated and avoid distractions. The experience was quite demoralising.

We can't move on from Tim's story without mentioning that his experience of social isolation might have been amplified by his young age, but we will discuss this later on in this chapter. For now, Tim's story shows how isolation can occur in any workplace setting. Even in a traditional office, connection isn't automatic – it depends on the environment and the systems that support it. This becomes particularly relevant when we examine remote work today, where we see organisations taking vastly different approaches to distributed work –and these differences significantly impact how connected their employees feel.

NOT ALL "REMOTE" IS CREATED EQUAL

It's clear that disconnection can occur in all settings, but for remote work setups, being intentional about creating an environment that values and encourages connection is especially important. Although this intention is also needed in other settings, when teams are colocated it can be easier to fall back on incidental connection, which is why the myth that remote workers are lonely prevails.

The context in which remote work takes place matters more than whether someone works remotely or not. Being a remote employee in a fully distributed company is fundamentally different from being the only remote worker in an office-first organisation. This distinction is important when we look at how organisations approach remote work policy.

Organisations that merely tolerate remote work while maintaining office-centric practices often create an environment where remote employees feel like second-class citizens. Without deliberate systems in place to ensure remote workers can participate fully in company life, disconnection becomes inevitable. In these situations, remote workers might miss information shared informally in the office, find themselves excluded from important discussions, or struggle to maintain visibility with decision-makers.

Once more, intentionality is the answer. This time the focus needs to be on designing equitable systems that support all employees, regardless of location. As Laurel Farrer wrote in a *Forbes*[3] article, "Remote workers shouldn't have to work twice as hard to be heard, seen, or considered for opportunities." Yet in many hybrid teams, those outside the office are at a disadvantage – not because they lack skills or ambition, but because the systems around them were built for in-person work.

In these contexts, Laurel's advice is to follow a remote-first approach to documentation, transparency, and asynchronous updates. In other words, communication that doesn't happen in real time but instead allows participants to respond within their work hours – whenever they may be. The same applies to meetings – defaulting to a shared online space, rather than inviting remote participants to an in-person meeting. This is not only a matter of fairness but can also ensure that remote team members don't feel informationally isolated or excluded from opportunities.

Beyond logistics, inclusion in remote teams is about belonging. Companies that embed equitable habits such as structured feedback loops, cross-team networking, and intentional recognition foster stronger connections and engagement. As Laurel notes, the goal is not just to make remote work possible but to ensure that "access, opportunity, and inclusion aren't dependent on proximity to an office."

The *Harvard Business Review* study we mentioned earlier supports this view, finding that a person can feel lonely in one job but not in another, suggesting that organisational context plays a significant role in employee connection. This aligns with Self-Determination Theory, which identifies relatedness – along with autonomy and competence – as a fundamental human need in the workplace. When organisations fail to support these needs through their environment and practices, employee engagement and motivation suffer.

The question isn't whether remote work causes loneliness, but rather how organisations can create environments that support meaningful connection for all employees, wherever they work. That's why we have dedicated a whole chapter in this book to what organisations can do to prevent people feeling disconnected from their organisation and colleagues.

THE UNIQUE CHALLENGES OF REMOTE TEAMS

The fact that remote work isn't the only setting where loneliness occurs doesn't diminish the reality that remote workers report significant feelings of isolation. In March 2024, Ringover, an AI-driven conversation platform for staffing and sales, surveyed 1,154 full-time employed US adults about their experiences and attitudes around loneliness at work.[4] They found that remote workers were the most likely to say that they "often" felt lonely at work (24%) compared to office workers (12.1%) and hybrid workers (8.6%).

We can't ignore the apparent tension between these stats and those that present office workers as being as lonely as remote workers, such as the Gallup study we previously cited. Whether remote workers would report less loneliness under different organisational policies or cultural norms, we can't say for sure.

What we do know is that while loneliness isn't exclusive to remote work, offices often provide us with physical environments to which we develop meaningful attachments. And although our connection to physical spaces may not be as profound as our bonds with people, it can still influence our sense of belonging.

On reading the first draft of this book, one of our friends offered this perspective:

"Our sense of belonging can be triggered or created by our material environment. Having a dedicated desk in an office was the old way. Then came the free desk approach which was much less personalised for an employee as there were no personal elements (frames, tags, pictures etc). Could this have an impact on our sense of belonging, which would then have an impact on our feeling of loneliness?"[5]

Beyond this attachment to material spaces, offices also provide us with the physical proximity that fosters spontaneous moments of connection throughout the day. Some of these interactions happen away from the work itself, while others emerge through the work. When we shift to remote settings, these moments don't occur by chance – we have to create them with intention.

Meetings are one of the places where casual connection naturally happens in the office. In face-to-face settings, there's often time before or after them for informal conversation. You don't plan for this to happen or put extra time in the meeting – it's just part of how these interactions naturally flow. This casual conversation might be the only time people get to catch up on what's happening in their colleagues' personal lives or hear about work achievements they're proud of. In the online space, you can't achieve that without being deliberate. People often end up having to specifically schedule time in the agenda for social chat, or it simply doesn't happen.

The same applies to making work visible, which we will cover further in Chapter 6. Remote set-ups require us to explicitly communicate everything from our daily progress and challenges to our thought processes and collaborative needs. Without this deliberate communication – and ideally, established team or organisational processes to support it – our collaborators might miss out on valuable information.

There's another challenge: remote workers are literally less visible than those who work next to each other. If somebody is going through a rough time, it's likely that when they come into a physical workspace, others will notice they're not well. In the remote space, this can easily be missed. We have to be more vigilant and listen for different kinds of cues. Have someone's chat messages been reduced in length? Has someone who was always the first to offer help to a colleague in need now gone quiet when others need a hand? We get to see much fewer physical cues, making it harder to spot when someone might need support.

THE ATTRACTION OF REMOTE FOR INTROVERTS

In the article "We're Still Lonely at Work", which we mentioned earlier, the authors found that introverts were more likely to be lonely at work than extroverts, even though they typically may be comfortable with more limited social interaction. Introverts tend to feel more energised by spending time alone or in low-stimulation environments, and may find extended social interaction draining – even if they enjoy it. That means you can be highly sociable and still be an introvert if solitude is what helps you recharge and do your best thinking.

Pilar is a good example of this. As an only child, she invested energy and effort into early friendships and she has been organising group activities all her life – both for work and for fun. However, when it comes to work, she can think of no better place than her desk at home. Pilar gets easily distracted by noise and activity around her – at conferences for example, she often needs to take short breaks on her own when the environment becomes overwhelming.

While introverts might be drawn to remote work because it provides their ideal working environment, this same preference for solitude might make them less likely to reach out to others. When you're comfortable being alone, it can sometimes take longer to recognise when you've become disconnected. You might be so content in your quiet, productive space that you forget to maintain those important social connections until loneliness has already set in. Without the ability to reconnect with team members or engage in social interactions, the once appealing solitude can turn into a source of emptiness and disconnection.

Brian Rhea, a developer, who, at the time of our podcast season, was creating a culture tool to help identify team connectedness, captured this paradox perfectly. "I was talking through that particular piece of the topic with a friend of mine, and joking, he said, 'Yeah, the first couple of months of working remote, you're like, nice, nobody taps me on the shoulder anymore. And then a year later you're like, huh, nobody is there to tap me on the shoulder anymore'. That little axiom there sums it up quite nicely."

That shoulder tap represents more than an interruption; it's often a catalyst for collaboration, an opportunity for mentorship, or a chance to solve problems together. When someone taps your shoulder in an office, they might be sharing an insight that sparks creativity, offering help with a challenge you've been stuck on, or creating a moment of connection that strengthens team bonds. While these interactions can sometimes disrupt focus, they also create valuable opportunities for growth and learning that need to be deliberately recreated in remote environments.

When we are absorbed in our work, we're in danger of reducing "work" to simply completing tasks as efficiently as possible. We can then miss out on the richness that comes from external input, creative problem-solving, and even shared experiences. Something as simple as taking a walk to clear your head or commiserating with colleagues about a challenging project can make work both easier and more effective. Deep, focused work is important, but it's most powerful when we've already gathered all our resources – including energy, focus, and confidence – which often come from our community connections.

While loneliness can affect any worker regardless of their location, remote workers face a unique challenge. Without the built-in connection points that physical workspaces provide, it's easier to slip into isolation without noticing. The very nature of remote work requires us to be more intentional about creating these vital touch points for collaboration, support, and shared experience.

SLOW CREEP

We could argue that self-awareness is more important in remote workers than those regularly visiting an office, and this includes understanding your mood.

Marcus Wermuth, who has been working as a remote manager for many years, and who we initially met when he was working for the distributed company Buffer, didn't notice how working from home was affecting him until he found himself surrounded by people.

"In 2018, I started public speaking, which is something I hadn't really done before. But at conferences, I got to meet people and I got to chat to people, and they were coming up to me, which was great, being more of an introvert. And in those moments, I realised, 'Oh, this is cool. I can talk to people'. And at retreats, when I met my coworkers, this was great. You could bond, you could build relationships. I started asking myself: 'When I'm at conferences, I feel so energised. When I'm at the retreat, I feel so energised. Why might that be?'

It was then I started to notice the effect of working from home in the long term."

The act of noticing changes in himself and then asking follow up questions is what eventually led Marcus to develop strategies around increasing virtual connection points with his team. (We'll come across some of these later on in Chapter 6 when we look at the role of the manager in fostering a sense of connection.)

The fact that these feelings creep up gradually, means it can be difficult to identify them as feelings of isolation, disconnection, and loneliness. That's why being self reflective is so important when changes in your behaviour or symptoms arise.

FACTORS THAT FUEL THE SLOW CREEP

But what about preventative measures? There are certain factors that may increase a person's likelihood of experiencing loneliness. And, just as working remotely doesn't automatically mean you'll feel disconnected, these factors are certainly not guarantees of loneliness. They're simply factors that could increase your risk.

"Some of these can be demographic factors," Dr. Holt-Lunstaad explained to our podcast listeners. "Those who live alone are more likely to be lonely. That doesn't necessarily mean that just because you live alone that you will be lonely, but it does increase your risk. Those who are unmarried are also at greater risk, but the flip side of that is that you can also feel lonely in a marriage.

The state of your physical health and mental health can also influence how likely you are to feel lonely. For example, those with mobility and communication impairments are also at risk. Those who have a harder time physically getting out into their community are going to be at greater risk, as are those with untreated hearing loss and language barriers.[6]

There is also evidence that loneliness, or the prevalence of loneliness, may be highest among younger adults relative to other groups. A possible explanation, when you consider loneliness as 'a discrepancy between one's actual level of social connection and one's desired level of social connection,' is that in younger phases of life we expect our social networks to be expanding and growing, whereas later in life the norm is for them to either be stable or to narrow somewhat. This is an example where our expectations can potentially have an impact on exaggerating or minimising these discrepancies."

Indeed, post-pandemic, we have often seen young people's experience of the workplace cited as a reason for encouraging (or forcing!) knowledge workers to go into the office. In our younger years, we often socialise with our colleagues, and begin to build our personal and professional networks. Unless an organisation is deliberately facilitating these connections online, it's easier for them to happen when people gather in an office.

Dr. Holt-Lunstad suggests that another point in time where we are at greater risk of loneliness are life transitions.

"Whether that is leaving home for the first time, or becoming a new parent, or divorce, or retirement, these life transitions are also potential triggers," she told us.

With this in mind, the transition to remote work itself could also be a risk factor to loneliness especially if you're transitioning at an individual level, rather than together with your team.

"If we can potentially help people as they transition, to really help mitigate that risk, that may be another touch point where we can help to reduce the risk of people entering into loneliness," Dr. Holt-Lunstad argues. "Because once someone becomes profoundly lonely, it's much more difficult to get out of that than to help reduce it early on or even prevent it. But oftentimes we may not know where people are at."

And this is the issue.

THE STIGMA OF LONELINESS

Even when we understand the risks of feeling lonely, and even if we keep an eye out for any symptoms, there is another factor that stops us from sharing these insights: shame.

If we constantly want to appear capable and committed to our work and our team, it can be extremely difficult to be open about times when we're struggling, and even more difficult to ask for help. This in turn can make us feel more disconnected, exacerbating the issue which could, if left unchecked, grow into a more chronic form of loneliness.

You can see where this is heading.

Masking due to shame also means managers might miss the signs of loneliness, which could otherwise trigger practical solutions like the redistribution of work or more regular check-ins with their team.

While we've made some progress in supporting mental health on a societal level, feelings of stigma or shame still hold people back. Admitting to problems that may be affecting our mental health, particularly when you're supposed to be enjoying your work or asserting yourself professionally, becomes more difficult. Unfortunately, this challenge is particularly relevant to remote work.

Despite a steady increase in remote work, with some studies suggesting around 70% of people work remotely at least once a week[7], there's still often a collective feeling of it being some special prize. Even after the pandemic, we still hear how employees are "allowed" to work from home, or presenting remote work as a perk. Within this frame of thinking, where you're supposed to be grateful for the flexibility you've been afforded, it's difficult to admit you may be struggling as a remote worker.

This was Asia Hundley's experience. Asia, who is originally from the United States, had several stints studying abroad in Spain as part of her University programme. Eventually, she decided to move permanently to Madrid and began looking for work. As her job hunting progressed, she came across a remote position offered by Shield GEO. "I felt it in my bones that it was the job for me," she told Bree when recording for our podcast season.

As she started working for a fully distributed company for the first time, Asia felt the tension of enjoying her time living abroad, while also missing her family and friends back home. It wasn't until she started reading articles about remote workers feeling lonely that she started to recognise similar feelings in herself. And because she had moved abroad, it was difficult to identify whether those feelings were "normal" as part of the transition, or something she should be paying attention to.

"In the beginning, everything's exciting, so you don't really focus on the sporadic feelings of loneliness. And because you're not sure how long you will stay abroad, you don't do anything to address them. Then once you are somewhere long enough where you feel like you could grow roots there, then you start to think about being away from your family, missing your friends, losing contact with a lot of people because of the time difference, and it's really hard to keep up with friends and keep those friendships alive."

It was only when she saw a post by Tim Burgess, her employer, that she started reflecting on her feelings. "In our chat for the entire company, Tim would post articles about how to cope with working remotely and the different challenges people faced". Reading those articles, Asia recognised she was experiencing some of the challenges described, and became more aware of how they were affecting her. She then looked out for more articles about other people's experiences, and, eventually, she reached out to her manager for help on adjusting her own environment.

Asia's experience highlights how important it is for organisations to normalise conversations about connection and belonging. When company leaders openly discuss these challenges, it helps break down the stigma that prevents people from seeking support. But beyond encouraging these conversations, there is much more organisations can do to support connection in distributed teams.

EVERYONE IS REMOTE

Given these unique challenges, remote teams need deliberate strategies to foster connection. However, the solution isn't as simple as recreating office behaviours in virtual spaces or implementing more tools and technologies. Instead, organisations need to rethink how they approach connection entirely.

Organisations should see themselves as remote-first if they have any remote employees at all. In the same way that people away from the central office – whether they're working from home or in a co-working space – are "remote", so are those who work in the office but collaborate with those who are not physically present. This shift in perspective will prevent organisations from operating as office-first companies that happen to have remote employees, rather than truly distributed organisations. It will prevent situations like managers only getting in touch with remote employees when there is an emergency, or when they are concerned with their performance at work.

When remote workers are not front of mind in an organisation's culture, it often leads to the emergence of formal or informal systems that prevent remote employees from feeling like they belong to the organisation, or from connecting with their colleagues as effectively as those who are office-based. Without the intentional design of processes, communication channels, and social opportunities, remote workers can easily become disconnected.

While in-person workplaces often rely on spontaneous interactions in physical spaces to build connection, online organisations need to identify these spaces and intentionally create opportunities for meaningful engagement. This doesn't mean scheduling every interaction, but rather creating an environment where connection can flourish naturally within a virtual context.

Understanding these fundamental principles is essential before we explore specific strategies and solutions. Only by acknowledging the unique nature of remote work – and its inherent challenges around connection – can organisations begin to build truly inclusive and engaging remote-first cultures.

We've mentioned many ways in which organisations can shift their perspective and adapt their environment to prevent disconnection from their employees. But ultimately, are they solely responsible for this shift? And, to what extent are managers and individual contributors also responsible? We address this in the next chapter.

SUMMARY

- Loneliness at work is not solely a remote work issue. It affects all types of work environments, including on-site and hybrid setups.

- Company culture and individual personality traits have a greater impact on loneliness than work location.

- Remote teams need to be intentional about creating opportunities for connection. This includes scheduling time for social interaction, making work visible (e.g. updating progress of tasks in shared boards, sharing your thinking and learnings, collaboration on documents), and being vigilant about noticing changes in colleagues' behaviour.

- Introverts may be drawn to remote work, but their preference for solitude can make them more susceptible to loneliness. They may need to be more proactive about maintaining social connections.

- It requires self-awareness and reflection to recognise signs of disconnection and loneliness.

- There is still a stigma associated with loneliness, which can prevent people from seeking help. Organisations need to normalise conversations about connection and belonging.

CONTINUING THE CONVERSATION

1. How can we ensure that remote team members don't have to work twice as hard to be heard, seen, or considered for opportunities?

2. How can we create more intentional opportunities for casual connection and social interaction within our remote team?

3. How might the personality traits or the personal circumstances of our team members influence their experience of loneliness at work? How can we tailor our approach to support diverse needs?

4

SHARING RESPONSIBILITY FOR CONNECTION

As we continue to unpack disconnection within the framework of remote workers and the organisations they work for, it feels important to discuss where the responsibility for this challenge lies.

Is it solely up to organisations and managers to ensure their teams feel connected? Or should individuals be tasked with self-monitoring and seeking out connection points beyond their immediate work tasks? More likely, it's a combination of the two, but how exactly should that play out to avoid these concerns falling through the cracks?

In this chapter, we examine these nuances including the concept of duty of care in a remote context, the role of intentional strategy in fostering connection, and how our environments impact our experience of life.

DEFINING ROLES AND RESPONSIBILITIES

In the Connection and Disconnection episode focusing on leadership,[1] Laurel Farrer defined work as "identifying a problem and developing a solution." From that foundation she then extrapolates management to mean "overseeing that production and ensuring the desired results are produced."

In other words, it's the individual's responsibility to complete the work that they've been hired to do, and it's the manager's responsibility to manage the overall workflow.

However, Laurel also said that we tend to relate this definition only to the tangible tasks, assignments and responsibility and forget about the intangible things that help us get there. Things like culture, psychological safety, trust, and ultimately, what we're discussing throughout this book – connection.

When Bree first started working as a writer she would often feel disappointed in her productivity or output when she had work days that revolved around tasks that weren't actually writing. While she understood days filled with emails, admin, meetings and the like were part of her job description and important to the overall progression of her assignments and tasks, Bree would often finish out the day feeling as if she hadn't done anything at all. At some point she had defined "work" somewhat narrowly as only the act of writing and any days where she didn't quite get there felt unproductive and not useful.

By focusing too much on the specific task of writing, Bree wasn't allowing those supporting tasks the time and attention they needed. In the end, her writing suffered.

In the same way, as we have already discussed in previous chapters, when we disregard efforts towards connection and other intangible support tasks, our productivity – or those more tangible work tasks – can suffer too.

THE NUANCED NATURE OF RESPONSIBILITY

While we can by now (we hope!) agree that connection within teams is an important – though somewhat intangible – part of work, discovering who is responsible for establishing and maintaining this connection isn't so straightforward.

Responsibility of even very concrete tasks between managers and employees is already quite nuanced. While Laurel's earlier definition of leadership splits many of the day-to-day tasks under these specific roles nicely, there are some that straddle both and some that don't quite seem to fit either.

An example of this might be deadlines. It's generally the manager's role to set the deadline and often they have a fairly good understanding of how long a certain task should take but individuals frequently have a much closer relationship to the actual steps required to complete the task, given they are the ones responsible for finishing it. While the manager is overseeing the overall workflow including the workload of each of their reports, it's the employee's responsibility to share when something has gone wrong or there is a hold up that could affect the deadline. The manager can then update the task or interrogate the delay. This feedback and collaboration between them is essential to the success of the task.

Connection is similar. Without an organisation that prioritises connection by allocating time, resources and training to fostering it, managers will have difficulty initiating exercises that promote connection with their teams, particularly if it's seen as taking time away from more 'important productive work'. If connection isn't prioritised at the organisational level, even if individuals can identify they feel disconnected from their manager or team, they won't have incentive to seek to reestablish this connection, and may even feel the need to move on from the company.

According to HubSpot's 2023 Hybrid Work Report titled "The Age of Connection", 60% of remote workers say that feeling connected to their organisation's mission or purpose influences their intent to stay in their role. That number is similar for hybrid (61%) and in-office workers (55%)[2,3].

Equally, without employee feedback, managers may be completely unaware of the true state of their team and miss out on the chance to make changes.

Put simply, while the roles in an organisation may be clearly defined, responsibility must be shared, as individuals often work in tandem for success.

Luckily when all parties take ownership it's a win-win. Courtney

Seiter, who has spent her career looking for ways of creating a healthy work culture, fully appreciates the need for a shared commitment.

"It just makes so much sense from a business point of view that you would want to make sure that the people who are creating your products – or whatever it is you make or produce – are doing okay and are able to keep doing their work in a way that feels sustainable. Strictly from a business point of view, your people are what make things happen for your company. So, if you don't take care of them, your long-term success is very much in peril."[4]

HOW OUR ENVIRONMENT IMPACTS OUR EXPERIENCE

The problem of disconnection in the setting of a remote team is that the lines are even more blurred. Work often occurs within someone's home and alongside other personal habits. If an individual hasn't left their apartment in weeks, worked from their couch and had all of their meals delivered, it's obvious they are responsible for those habits. But what if they were sent to another city or country on a project? Or the company decided to close down the office and ask everyone to work from home? Or, as is often the case for remote workers, were onboarded without any training, education or resources on how to stay safe while working remotely?

For Tim Burgess, even though an individual is choosing to apply for a position, the power in this relationship is skewed towards the employer.

"When we're hiring people, we're hiring them into a circumstance that *we* create, not them," he said. "And so if we're hiring somebody in a situation where they're not going to have colleagues sitting next to them, they might not even have colleagues in their own time zone – we do bear responsibility for that."

It is well-established that our environments play a big part in how we feel and how easy it is to perform certain tasks. This clearly goes beyond our physical setting and includes systems, policies, culture and other infrastructure that contribute to our experience.

Dr. Holt-Lunstaad puts it this way: "When there are factors in the environment that systematically put people in situations that increase potential risk – whether those are policies that are in place or the way our physical environment creates barriers – that makes it more difficult."

In practice this looks like finding it easy to ride your bike in Amsterdam but much harder to do so in Utah.

"When I lived in the Netherlands, I rode my bike every single day, many days in the rain. It was very easy, because the environment was set up for it. There were bike trails everywhere, and I felt very safe, because the paths were separated from the cars," Dr. Holt-Lunstaad shared. "Then I come back to Utah, and I am bound and determined to do the same thing. But my physical environment makes it much more difficult. I don't have designated bike lanes, so it would mean going in traffic, and there are massive mountains and hills that make biking much harder."

Our environment matters

In the same way, connecting with teammates, participating in meetings, or gathering the information needed to complete tasks might fall under your responsibility as an individual contributor, but if your environment isn't set up to support or facilitate this, it can make this particularly difficult, or even impossible.

Marcus Wermuth, who regularly invests time and energy in his own leadership development, sees this playing out in scenarios where individuals may not feel safe to share that they are struggling.

"There's a responsibility for individuals to share or bring it up if they can. But ultimately that comes back to: Is the culture safe?" he said.

We know by now that so much of culture and behaviour is picked up almost incidentally. So while it may be company policy to have open communication about challenges or concerns, if your team doesn't see this value playing out or demonstrated in the leadership, it's unlikely it'll be adopted company-wide, even if logically it's the right thing to do.

"I think it's really useful to think about the different ways in which some of these systematic practices or policies, or even our physical environment, are set up. That in turn influences those individual choices," Julianne said.

LEGAL RESPONSIBILITY OR DUTY OF CARE

The responsibility we have discussed here, for the most part, speaks to the social obligations of our roles, answering questions like "What does it mean to be a manager?" and "What do we, as colleagues, owe each other in the workplace?"

While our answers to these questions may feel instinctual, there are no hard and fast rules and our responses are likely to change person to person and organisation to organisation.

But are there any legal obligations associated with supporting employees? And if there are, how does working remotely affect this?

Tara Vasdani, the principal lawyer at Remote Law Canada, shared her insight on the podcast from an Ontario perspective, which is where her firm is based.

Tara said employers have a legal duty to create a safe workplace for their employees.

Often this refers to having a remote employee remove any physical safety hazards, like electrical cords in walkways. But, according to Tara, it can refer to mental wellbeing too.

"When you're thinking about caring for your remote employees from a legal health and safety perspective, employee wellness matters too. Sometimes the lines can be blurred because employers tend to think that when employees are in their own space, they don't need to be cared for. And it's a misconception, and it frankly, shouldn't happen.

One thing that I encourage remote employers to be mindful of is that, for example, in Ontario, under our Human Rights Code, employers are not permitted to discriminate based on disability. Mental and physical disabilities are treated the same in Ontario, and therefore, you can very well have an employee that has a "safe and healthy" workspace, meaning, it is free and clear of trip hazards, but has also been neglected or not cared for. All of a sudden, this employee is suffering from depression or anxiety or other mental health related symptoms, and you could very quickly be facing a lawsuit for discrimination by not accommodating them, or ensuring that you are minimising some of the conditions they're suffering from to the greatest extent."

Tara suggests seeking legal advice when setting up remote or hybrid work approaches to understand the obligations in your particular state or territory. From there it's a good idea to create a robust framework or health and safety policy that considers wellness holistically.

THE INDIVIDUAL'S ROLE

It's clear how interconnected the responsibility for connection really is. The environment, culture and internal policies are generally set and upheld by leaders in the organisations. There may even be some legal responsibility to maintain a safe environment for work, which could include mental and social wellbeing. Individual managers also play an important part in creating a sense of psychological safety for their teams and are often relied upon to lead by example and "live out" the values of a company. (We'll come back to psychological safety in Chapter 6.)

With this framework in place, connection should be fairly straightforward. But, of course, it's never really that simple. All the careful planning in the world won't matter if an individual isn't willing to participate.

Isabel Collins is a Belonging and Culture consultant. Since 2014, she's focused on fostering a sense of belonging within a workplace. Isabel agrees that employers and organisations have a duty of care to provide support and resources that cater to both safety and wellbeing. However, she admits this is multi-faceted.[5]

"Belonging really is multi-way. It's not about command and control, top down. So, although there is the responsibility of duty of care, you can't tell someone to belong."

There is a point where the role of the manager and the company at large must finish and the individual must take accountability.

Marcus agrees.

"I think there needs to be a line where managers then say, 'Okay, listen, I can help you until here, but then you should either see a professional or chat to your family or your friends to figure this out more.' Ultimately, there's a point where you can't help that person anymore. You can help them discover it, but you can't fix it all."

This boundary acknowledges that while workplace support is important, some issues require professional help or the support of family and friends. It also helps protect managers from taking on responsibilities beyond their expertise or role, while ensuring employees get the kind of support they need.

BUILDING COLLECTIVE RESPONSIBILITY

Even when we agree that organisations should utilise systems to support connection, we seem to be setting up these organisational systems too late in the game. This may be because most organisations grow organically and the needs of a two person team are different to one that's made up of 100, 200 or 300 people. Or it could be the case that an external event (like a pandemic) has forced employees to set up new systems in a rush.

It's also likely that developing rules around communication might not be something team members consider until they start running into problems. This is often the case with teams moving from the office to remote: they assume they can use online tools in the same ways they did in person. So while it's best to establish clear guidelines for using online tools as early as possible, these examples show that there needs to be room to adjust and evolve over time.

One way out of this is to bring team members into these discussions to allow them to create their own guidelines, ones that will actually be beneficial to their individual needs. In this way, the responsibility is shared in a way that empowers each team member to make decisions that have a direct, positive impact on how they experience their work. (We will expand on this idea when we talk about team agreements in Chapter 6.)

Building collective responsibility

When Shield GEO was developing its values as a company the leadership team incorporated various input sessions from the entire team. These were varied and staggered allowing different forms of collaboration including surveys, small-group ideation meetings and feedback opportunities. Once decided on, the team's anecdotes and quotes were used to tell the 'values story'. Because the team was included from the start it meant leadership didn't have to convince anyone to "buy-in". Not only were the agreed values something the team innately aligned with because it was their stories that helped build them, but the project of deciding together built a connection to these values and to each other.

You can see the application on a smaller scale. When a team works together to create their own guidelines, not only is it a better reflection of who they are and their work styles but the process builds bonds to the work, their manager and the rest of their teammates.

LEVERAGING TECHNOLOGY

When we talk about responsibility, it can sometimes come across as someone having to take on extra work. And with all the information shared so far, we can't blame you for thinking along those lines. Prioritising connection takes effort.

But there is some good news for remote teams. Given remote worker's reliance, interest in, and ease with technology, we think they might be in a unique position to address issues of disconnection. The technology and practices remote workers utilise in their daily work lives actually have the power to connect us and even take some of that burden of the "extra intention".

Pilar used to teach in a drama school for a couple hours a week. Sometimes she would turn up to find out that her class had been cancelled and nobody had told her. This information was probably circulated via pigeonholes or word of mouth and not having access to that information made her feel disconnected from her team because no one had thought, 'Oh, we better tell Pilar, because she has a class tomorrow.'

Imagine the 2025 equivalent of this story, where teams all have access to an online noticeboard. Changes in schedules are usually posted so no one has to think about who to tell because everyone has a responsibility to check and be involved in those conversations.

In some ways, technology removes some organisational effort (like someone having to remember to inform an individual that their class was cancelled) because there's a system in place that acts as a safety measure. No one falls through the cracks because, with the system in place, the responsibility is shared.

As we can see, there are no real clear cut answers here. The proportion of responsibility is likely to look different, company to company, but we don't think that that should deter us from doing the important work of discovery. We know that self reflection is key, but we also know that setting up a company that has the ability to function remotely is necessary too. Systems can help provide structure, but every individual has different needs. And while this can be messy at times, we think wrestling to work it out is incredibly worthwhile.

That's why we've structured the next four chapters to address each level of responsibility: what organisations can do at a systemic level, how managers can support their teams, and steps individuals can take to protect their own wellbeing in a remote environment.

SUMMARY

- The division of responsibility between managers and employees is nuanced, even for concrete tasks. This shared responsibility model also applies to the more intangible aspects of connection.

- Duty of care is a legal obligation that requires organisations to provide a standard of reasonable care to avoid foreseeable harm to others.

- Individuals also have a responsibility to speak up when they're struggling, though this relies on managers creating a safe space for such conversations to occur.

- Belonging is not a top-down approach; it requires participation from both the employer and the employee. While employers have a duty of care, individuals also need to take accountability.

- Having rules creates a structure where everyone knows where to start and who to connect with. But, while systems can provide structure, every individual has different needs.

- There are no clear-cut answers regarding the proportion of responsibility; it may vary from company to company. However, the work of discovering what works best is worthwhile.

CONTINUING THE CONVERSATION

1. To what extent do our team members feel that our work environment supports and facilitates connection, and what specific changes could be made to improve it?

2. How can we create a more psychologically safe space where team members feel comfortable speaking up about their struggles and challenges without fear of negative consequences?

3. How can we strike a balance between organisational support and individual accountability in fostering connection within our team?

5
ORGANISATIONAL SUPPORT

I n the previous chapter, we wrestled with the concept of responsibility for connection within an organisation. Building on that foundation, these next three chapters focus on the practical strategies that can be employed to foster connection in remote teams. We've taken a two-pronged approach: one that addresses both organisational structures and individual managerial practices.

Organisational strategies, which are the focus of this chapter, encompass the broader, company-wide initiatives that create the framework for connection. For example, establishing shared values, implementing communication structures, and providing resources that support employee wellbeing and engagement. These strategies set the tone for the entire company and create an environment where connection can flourish.

Managerial tactics, on the other hand, focus on the day-to-day practices that team leaders can employ to nurture connection within their immediate sphere of influence. These include regular check-ins, fostering open communication, and tailoring approaches to individual team members' needs. Managers play a crucial role as the bridge between organisational policies and individual employees, translating broad strategies into personalised practices – which is why they're the focus of the next two chapters.

While we've separated these strategies for clarity, in practice, they often overlap and intertwine. What's more, in small organisations, the only person above you in the hierarchy might be the CEO, and some businesses are small enough to function as one team.

DEFINING SHARED VALUES AND PURPOSE

Since its founding in 2010, Buffer has operated as a fully distributed organisation, embracing transparency and flexibility as core principles. This commitment to remote work has allowed the organisation to cultivate a diverse, global workforce while developing innovative strategies for maintaining connection and culture across digital spaces.

Buffer's commitment to transparency goes beyond its organisation - it was one of the first companies to share through its Open Culture Blog how its team was building the business and their approach to remote work. Since then, they've provided much needed inspiration and ideas for experimentation to distributed teams.

With this background of experience and intentionality, Buffer's insights into fostering connection in remote settings are particularly valuable. Courtney Seiter shared how, during her time at Buffer, she and the leadership team were deliberate about defining their internal value system since the company's inception. "We've been very intentional with our culture throughout almost all of that time, almost from the very beginning, we've tried to be very specific and explicit about the values that guide us."

These values, such as defaulting to transparency, showing gratitude, and practicing reflection, serve to unify Buffer's diverse team.

Of course, it's important to recognise that not every company will share these values or have the ability to embrace or implement such a high degree of transparency in their culture. Various factors, including industry regulations, competitive concerns, or established organisational norms, may limit the extent of transparency possible. However, this doesn't negate the importance of clarity and intentionality in defining company values. In fact, for organisations where full transparency isn't feasible, it becomes even more important to articulate clearly what can be shared, what cannot, and why. This honesty about the limits of transparency can itself foster trust and connection.

The key is to acknowledge the reality of an organisation's culture and build connection strategies that work within those parameters, rather than trying to force a one-size-fits-all approach. By doing so, companies can still create an environment of trust and belonging, even if it looks different from the highly transparent models of companies like Buffer.

PROVIDING RESOURCES AND SUPPORT

Organisations often ensure that employee handbooks, policies, and other useful documents are readily accessible online. Why not also provide easily available resources for employees who may be experiencing loneliness? As we've seen, individuals experiencing feelings of disconnection or loneliness may be reluctant to openly seek assistance, so it's helpful to provide resources they can access on their own.

Within these resources, it's a good idea to include Employee Assistance programmes, access to mental health resources, counselling services, and peer support groups, as well as guides to help recognise the signs of loneliness. It's important to remind employees about the existence of these support systems just as frequently as promoting other kinds of benefits, such as the latest discount partner programme.

As an example, one of Bree's previous employers provided a subscription to Calm, a meditation app offering a range of mental health and wellness services from guided meditations to sleep support. The platform covers a wide array of topics, allowing employees to address specific challenges they might be facing, whether work-related or personal.

Part of an organisation's wellbeing strategy could also include integrating reminders about wellbeing and connection resources into regular company communications, not just during times of crisis. This can help normalise the use of these resources and the conversation around mental health wellbeing in the organisation.

BUILDING A CULTURE OF CONNECTION

While teams will have their own practices and rituals which enable their team members to connect regularly, there is also value in organisations making "belonging" part of their ongoing people strategy. Here are some of the activities and initiatives we've picked up from our guests, and others.

1. **Video gatherings**: fostering social connections and face-to-face interactions.

For fully distributed organisations video gathering are a common way to intentionally create space for connection. These gatherings can revolve around serious topics or be more lighthearted and fun. The first time Pilar came across them was when she started working for Happy Melly. She knew that if she wanted to catch up with people in the company she never had the opportunity to collaborate with, Thursdays at 5.30pm CET was the time to log online. The discussions would emerge organically with whomever was there – no facilitation, no topics, no structure. This worked well because usually only 5 or 6 people would turn up, as there were only 12 people working for the organisation. Larger organisations tend to need more structure, which can be achieved through the use of breakout rooms, and by segmenting the meetings into interests, by having Book Clubs for example.

This casual format allows team members to see colleagues they might not interact with regularly, helping to maintain a sense of community across the organisation. It's an opportunity to catch up, share experiences, and maintain the social fabric of the company despite the physical distance. Many companies find making these drop-ins optional to attend helpful as it allows individuals to choose when and how they connect with their teams.

2. Online water coolers: creating an asynchronous virtual space for casual, spontaneous interactions.

This one is incredibly popular. Channels in organisation's chat-like platforms dedicated to social banter go from the classic #watercooler and #social to #random #chitchat and #funny[1]. At Shield GEO, they even had a channel called #grumbling, acknowledging that all social sharing doesn't always have to be "fun".

Bree, while not always an active contributor to the channel herself, found that complaints posted there naturally led to meaningful follow-up conversations – checking in about how construction was progressing or whether wifi issues had been resolved. Encouraging casual conversations and non-work-related discussions helps create spontaneous interactions that can shine light on people in different ways, and help them find social points of connection. Even when conversations didn't progress, it can simply be validating to have someone commiserate annoyances, even if there's no real solution.

3. Structured networking: facilitating connections between team members who might not regularly interact.

When you work for a distributed organisation, it's often difficult to meet people outside of your immediate team. Like most things in the remote space, if you don't create a process for something to happen, it won't happen at all. That's why many teams and organisations have implemented systems for randomly pairing people across the organisation. These pairings are designed to encourage short, casual conversations between colleagues who might not typically work together.

Pilar first came across this practice around 2018, while reading the blog of the project management tool, Trello. The article explained how Trello's (at the time) 40-person distributed team used one of the company's own boards to pair people across the organisation. One person was responsible for creating random pairs every two weeks which would then lead to a 15 minute meeting to have a chat. The pairs would then make a few notes in their "card", as a way of sharing with the rest of their colleagues some of the things they'd talked about. The practice of randomly pairing people up has become common in distributed organisations, and has been automated through apps like Donut.

There are other ways in which people within an organisation can get to know each other.

One activity that has stayed in Bree's mind years after working with Shield GEO, was the ongoing use of the Know Your Team tool. Through the app, Shield GEO employees had the opportunity to ask questions that were sent to the entire company to answer. These questions were sent three times a week, and were split into categories covering get-to-know-you icebreakers and more company-focused questions that employees might have not known where else to ask. A range of different questions were distributed to the entire organisation via email, including personal-type queries like, "What song have you listened to most this year?" and, "How do you like your eggs?" to more work-focused ones like, "How could our benefits package improve?" or "Should we be adding new channels of communication?". The answers were then populated into Slack (a chat-based collaboration tool) where team members could comment and interact. In practice, it gave foundations for further conversation in Donut calls or other meetings, as well as providing some tidbits that Bree still remembers!

While this might not come naturally to everyone, there are ways of introducing newcomers to the concept of online networking, so that it's seen as a key part of the company's culture. For example, every new hire at GitLab has to schedule at least five coffee chats during their onboarding[2].

In a way, these activities also take care of "information isolation", a form of disconnection that comes from being physically removed from the informal information flow that naturally occurs in an office environment. Rather than feeling socially isolated, information isolation stems from not knowing what's happening across the organisation due to missing out on casual conversations and updates that typically occur in person. Structured networking can help address this.

4. **Mastermind programme**: providing deep, ongoing support and connection for employees.

While random pairing has been set up for swift interactions focused on social connection, some individuals will benefit from being helped to develop different kinds of relationships, focused more on growing at work.

Mastermind Programmes are those where employees are matched

with a colleague outside their immediate work team but at a similar career stage. These pairs meet regularly for in-depth conversations, and the relationship is designed to be a safe space where employees can share their achievements, anxieties, workplace challenges, and even personal issues. While it's not meant to replace professional therapy, it provides a confidant and support system within the company. This kind of programme helps combat isolation by creating strong, meaningful connections between employees who might otherwise never interact closely.

5. **Co-working space membership:** supporting employees in combating isolation by working outside their homes.

As we've previously mentioned, when remote workers feel isolated, the answer to their disconnection doesn't always lie within the organisation - sometimes it's somewhere else in their lives.

Many organisations that don't have office premises recognise remote work is not just working from home, and support their employees who prefer alternative working spaces. Paying for co-working membership, or even paying for coffee consumed in a café, are both ways of recognising that home-based work can be isolating, and some people need to work elsewhere occasionally, or regularly. The company Remote, for example, offers their entire global workforce of over 1,000 people a monthly stipend towards the cost of an external working space. They do this in the belief that "doing so helps our employees live better, more productive lives and gives them the flexibility they need to do their best work"[3].

By working from a co-working space, employees can enjoy a change of scenery, potentially meet new people, and maintain a clearer separation between work and home life. This option provides the benefits of human interaction and a professional environment while maintaining the flexibility of remote work.

· · ·

6. **Emphasis on asynchronous communication**: ensuring inclusion of team members across all time zones in communication and decision-making.

Promoting asynchronous communication can help by breaking down barriers of time and geography. Asynchronous communication can happen in chats, project management tools, text documents, email, and in video or audio recordings. It allows team members across different time zones and schedules to participate fully in discussions and decision-making processes, ensuring no one is left out due to timing constraints. For example, important discussions might be held in shared documents with extended comment periods, rather than in real-time meetings. This can help prevent situations where employees in certain time zones feel like they're always "catching up" or missing out on key conversations.

At an organisational level, this also means not always relying on real-time meetings or presentations for senior leadership to convey information, but having a mixture of recorded and live channels, as well as combining audio and video with text.

Asynchronous communication also helps organisations where schedules overlap. Project management platforms, shared documents, and thoughtful messaging systems can all help create a more level playing field. It gives those who prefer to process information before responding the time and space to contribute meaningfully. This inclusivity leads to a diversity of perspectives and ideas that might otherwise be lost in the rapid-fire nature of synchronous meetings.

7. **Off-site retreats:** intentional in-person gatherings.

Remote workers particularly value off-site retreats as an opportunity to spend quality time with their colleagues away from daily work pressures. Remote employees, who rarely visit the office or who work for fully remote companies, tend to express more enthusiasm for these gatherings than their hybrid or office-based counterparts – perhaps because they offer a unique chance to deepen relationships through shared experiences and informal conversations[4].

In one of our podcast episodes, Asia Hundley mentioned drawing "a lot of energy" from the Shield GEO retreat in Thailand[5], while Courtney says that these gatherings are great for team members to "see faces you haven't seen in a while, just to get a little bit of social time."

Some companies use these in-person gatherings as part of their onboarding process. Having worked with a wide range of organisations, Laurel Farrer has noticed that "a lot of distributed companies say, 'come on site for the first two to three weeks of your job, get to know the team, get to know the processes, and then you can work remotely after that.'"

Although having principles and activities like the above will help most people, it's important to recognise that feelings of isolation can stem from various factors and affect individuals differently. It's therefore important to find personalised solutions when an employee expresses feelings of disconnection. Courtney shared some more examples of how she dealt with this at Buffer. For instance, if an engineer was feeling isolated, the company would arrange regular pair programming sessions to increase collaboration and social interaction. For employees who feel disconnected due to their geographic location, Buffer might help them connect with local professional organisations or tech meetups[6].

THE RIGHT INTERNAL WORK ENVIRONMENT

Much of our sense of belonging and connection stems from the interactions and collaboration we experience within our work environment. Ensuring that employees are satisfied with their work and have the autonomy to manage their tasks can significantly reduce stress and prevent feelings of detachment from their work and colleagues.

"Providing adequate equipment and technology" might not be the first thing that comes to mind when thinking about how to prevent our people from feeling disconnected, but, how close do you feel to someone in a meeting when their audio is poor? Or how much do you feel a sense of belonging to your team, when you can't find the latest answer to your burning question buried in a discussion thread?

With this in mind, we wanted to share the recommendations from a recent meta-study[7] from SASTRA University in India which assessed the effects of remote work on employee productivity and wellbeing.

The study examines how factors such as job satisfaction, technological accessibility, and social support, influence employee productivity and wellbeing. As well as supporting much of what we have already covered, like the importance of designing opportunities for social support and creating environments for social communication, the authors have other recommendations.

Provide adequate resources and technology

The study found that a lack of access to necessary tools and resources was associated with increased stress and decreased productivity. This suggests that organisations should ensure employees have access to the necessary resources and technology to perform their tasks efficiently, including having reliable internet connections, necessary software, and hardware.

Job autonomy

Allowing employees a degree of autonomy in how they perform their tasks can lead to increased job satisfaction and productivity. Trusting employees to manage their workload and make decisions can also reduce feelings of isolation and increase engagement.

Flexible work schedules

Flexible work schedules were also found to be key in maintaining employee productivity and wellbeing. Employees who had more control over their work schedules and tasks reported better job satisfaction and lower levels of stress.

This flexibility addresses the diverse ways people find connection in their lives. While most organisations aim for employees to find meaning and connection at work, it's important to recognise that individual circumstances, job roles, and personalities can mean that their sense of belonging is found in their communities or homes. By providing flexibility at work, they can find opportunities to connect with others outside of work, bringing that happiness and fulfilment back into the work environment.

And last, but definitely not least:

Regular communication

Maintaining regular and transparent communication with remote workers can help them feel connected and supported. This includes regular updates on company news, team meetings, and one-on-one check-ins with managers.

In fact, a study carried out amongst Taiwanese remote workers in mid-2021 during the Taiwanese government's remote work advocacy to restrict the spread of Covid-19, showed that timely and accurate information reduces loneliness and positively affects wellbeing[8].

EVALUATING YOUR CONNECTION STRATEGIES

As there is no one-size-fits-all, and changes in context affect how teams and individuals work, managers and their teams need to continuously evaluate their connection processes. Even if an organisation's core remains stable, the context and people within it evolve. An intervention that works in one scenario, might be of no benefit when things change.

This is why implementation is only part of the process. As with any initiative, understanding the real impact of these strategies requires measuring their effectiveness and evaluating their outcomes. This involves actively seeking feedback from employees, tracking engagement levels, and assessing the overall effects on individual and team wellbeing.

Without these feedback loops, it's difficult to know whether connection efforts are truly making a difference or need adjustment. When we look at connection through the organisational lens rather than the team lens, we see that what works well for one team, may not work for another.

Furthermore, the measurement of success should go beyond simple metrics. While tracking participation in events and activities or usage of online resources can provide useful data points, it's equally important to explore the qualitative aspects of connection. This can be done through incorporating regular surveys or feedback sessions to gauge how employees feel about the connection opportunities offered.

Are these opportunities seen as authentic and meaningful?

Do they help employees feel more valued and supported?

Taking a more holistic approach to evaluation helps managers gain a deeper understanding of the complex nature of connection and continuously improve their strategies to create a truly inclusive and connected workplace.

After reading the first draft of this book, Tim Burgess recommended that we take a look at a blog post written by Jessica Reeder, Upwork's Director of Remote Organisational Effectiveness. In her piece, she suggests that engagement surveys should include items such as "I have the information I need to do my job". While not explicitly a culture metric, this data point can become a critical indicator, as declining scores here can undermine broader cultural initiatives.

Jessica also mentions that psychological safety metrics reflect managers' remote leadership capabilities, noting that improvements in manager effectiveness should correlate with enhanced psychological safety. Finally, she highlights that communication systems should embody an organisation's values – when systems prioritise inclusion, transparency, and trust, employees typically report stronger connections to the company's mission[9].

These organisational measurements provide a valuable framework, but implementing effective connection strategies ultimately happens at the team level. While organisational policies and culture create the foundation for connection within remote teams, managers serve as important bridges between company initiatives and individual employees. Their regular interactions with team members put them in a unique position to support connection.

Along with a strategy and individual responsibility, managers can help foster an environment where authentic connections can flourish. However, this requires specific skills and approaches that might differ from traditional management practices. "Helping team members feel connected to their team and organisation" should become a core leadership practice and part of an organisation's leadership development objectives in remote/hybrid, or remote-first organisations.

As always, it's not just a question of borrowing "best practices" from successful remote companies. For managers to see themselves as enablers of human connection, it requires a new mindset, familiarity with the different ways people connect, and a high degree of self-awareness. This can be particularly challenging for new managers or those just beginning to lead remote teams.

So this is where we turn to next.

SUMMARY

- Defining your organisations shared values and purpose helps to form the basis for connection strategies that fit your specific culture.

- Providing online loneliness resources such as Employee Assistance.

- Programmes, mental health resources, counselling services and peer support groups alongside other benefits provides an easy way for employees to access support.

- There are a number of practices that promote connection among distributed teams.

- Implementation is one step in the process, evaluating the success of processes and practices is just as important.

CONTINUING THE CONVERSATION

1. How well do our team members understand and align with our organisation's shared values and purpose? What steps can we take to strengthen this alignment?

2. What specific social opportunities does our organisation offer to foster connection among employees, and how can we ensure that these opportunities are accessible and appealing to all team members?

3. In what ways can we leverage technology to create a more inclusive and engaging remote environment, and what steps can we take to prevent technology overload?

4. How can we ensure that teams' communication practices are inclusive of all members, regardless of their time zone or communication preferences?

5. How do we currently evaluate the effectiveness of our connection-building initiatives, and what metrics can we use to gain a deeper understanding of their impact on employee wellbeing and team cohesion?

6. In what ways might our team or organisation be inadvertently creating an environment where remote employees feel like second-class citizens? What steps can we take to address this?

7. What steps can our organisation take to ensure that it is meeting its duty of care obligations to support the wellbeing of remote employees, including addressing mental health and social connection?

6

MANAGER SUPPORT: CONNECTING THROUGH THE WORK

While many factors contribute to fostering a connected remote team, managers play an important role in this process, sitting at the intersection of organisational culture, team dynamics, and individual employee experiences. In this chapter and the next, we cover how managers can open up the conversation around loneliness, how teamwork can be structured to enable connection and how they can support individuals. We've written the chapters primarily for those in official team leadership positions, however, team members looking for ways to improve collaboration will find plenty of inspiration here too.

THE ROLE OF THE MANAGER

Managers shape an employee's experience of the workplace in significant ways – with Gallup research suggesting that they account for at least 70% of the variance in team engagement.[1] As it turns out, recent research confirms that managers also influence employees' sense of connection through their behaviours and leadership approach.

More directly, research that took place in 2024, involving 531 employees in Chinese public sectors, showed that when leaders empower their team members, employees develop greater confidence in managing their wider responsibilities, which helps reduce feelings of isolation at work. This relationship appears stronger when leaders and team members engage in high-quality conversations, suggesting that empowering leadership approaches are more effective at combating workplace loneliness when combined with meaningful communication between managers and their reports.

Furthermore, in 2024 Gallup suggested that "intentional planning" and "structured engagement" are fundamental to preventing isolation in distributed teams – all of which a manager is perfectly positioned to carry out.

So what makes managers uniquely positioned to diminish workplace loneliness?

1. Managers have formal authority

No matter how flat the organisation, how collaborative a manager is, or how autonomous team members feel, employees will take their cues from managers as to what behaviours are acceptable or not. Leadership behaviour tends to influence team norms.

Additionally, as someone with formal authority, managers can make decisions around people's schedules and commitments, which, as we saw in the previous section, can help prevent loneliness. They also hold employees accountable for their performance.

2. Managers have an overview of the team's work and process

It's a manager's job to know how everyone's work fits together. Of course, all team members need to understand how their work and tasks interconnect, but having an overall view of how the team operates is a manager's responsibility.

By intentionally structuring work processes and interactions, managers can create natural opportunities for collaboration and meaningful engagement. Redesigning a team's work to strengthen relationships and foster a sense of belonging is a powerful strategy for building connection in a remote team – but it is often overlooked.

3. Managers are responsible for team members' development and wellbeing

Managers are expected to have regular individual interactions with team members, formally or informally. These conversations go beyond work performance and professional aspirations; they present the opportunity to understand team members as whole individuals, including their personal challenges, motivations, and overall well being.

Regular one-on-ones should be a safe space where team members feel comfortable sharing their experiences, including any feelings of isolation or disconnection. (We cover one-on-ones in the next chapter.)

4. Managers are formally and informally connected to the rest of the organisation

Managers are often part of a leadership team or regularly talk to those in other parts of the organisation. This makes them a good source of information on what's going on in the organisation and positions them as potential "connectors" – people who help broker relationships between team members and others in the organisation. This connecting role increases the chances of team members forming meaningful relationships outside their immediate team and understanding how their work contributes to larger organisational goals.

Given these four points, we can see how manager and team leader behaviour set the tone for an entire team. This brings us to the importance of role modelling. By demonstrating the behaviours and attitudes managers want to see in their teams, they can create a culture of openness, vulnerability, and connection.

THE IMPACT OF ROLE MODELLING ON PSYCHOLOGICAL SAFETY

"The first thing I do is try to bring my humanity into my role," Teresa Douglas shared in one of our original podcast episodes, perfectly capturing this role modelling behaviour.

"Recently we experienced some restructuring, and some people from a different part of the company joined our team. In my first email to them, I sent a picture of me with my kids and I talked about what I do outside of work, and the fact that I play guitar badly, and that I run, and that I'm happy to meet with people, you know, crack little jokes.

And right away I had a couple of responses, "Oh, I do that thing too", or, "Oh, my kids are also that age". I felt that immediate connection with them because I provided excuses for them to talk to me. It's about bringing humanity to your role.

As managers, we have to do that. We have to recognise the power dynamic at play. My direct reports get paid if they do a good job, and I'm one of the people that decides if they're doing a good job. So if they get the feeling that I'm in their corner, that I'm a basically friendly presence, when I start connecting with them it's easier for them to open up. Since we're in that power position, we have to offer the first vulnerability."[2]

Teresa has been managing people for over a decade and she regularly shares her insights publicly, including on her blog *Living la Vida Remota*. The above reflections demonstrate one of the ways in which managers can actively build psychological safety: through showing vulnerability. By acknowledging the inherent power dynamic and choosing to share personal details first, Teresa showed what opening up might look like. Her strategy of sharing lighthearted personal information – from musical hobbies to family life – creates natural connection points while showing that bringing one's whole self to work is not just acceptable, but welcomed. When leaders take the first step in showing vulnerability, they signal to their teams that it's safe to do the same.

We've already discussed how challenging it can be for people to open up about feeling disconnected, even when they've recognised it themselves. To encourage our team members to be open about these feelings, we need to create an environment where people feel comfortable expressing themselves. This concept is commonly known as psychological safety.

More broadly, psychological safety refers to the shared belief within a team that it's safe to take interpersonal risks, such as speaking up with ideas, questions, concerns, or mistakes, without fear of negative consequences to one's self-image, status, or career.

This concept was pioneered by Harvard professor Amy Edmondson and has since become an often-quoted element of high-performing teams. In fact, in 2022 meQ[3] carried out a Member Research Report[4], which surveyed around 3,900 employees to show its importance across different work environments. Drawing on Edmondson's original seven-item scale, the study measured key behaviours that indicate psychological safety in teams:

- Feeling safe to take risks within the team
- Being able to raise problems and tough issues
- Confidence that teammates would not deliberately undermine efforts
- Not having mistakes held against you
- Finding it easy to ask team members for help
- Feeling accepted and respected when being different
- Valuing and respecting each other's contributions

MeQ's survey results reported substantially higher psychological safety in remote/hybrid employees than their on-site counterparts. Remote/hybrid employees were 66% less likely to feel mistakes were held against them, 56% less likely to experience rejection for differences, and 36% less likely to find asking for help difficult. They also reported greater comfort discussing difficult topics, taking risks, and feeling valued.

The researchers proposed several explanations for the difference between remote/hybrid employees and those working in the office. These included the idea that online environments may need more intentional check-ins from managers, and that digital collaboration tools could provide a psychological buffer that makes it safer to speak up.

While these findings on psychological safety are promising, creating a safe team environment alone may not be enough. Even in psychologically safe environments, there are often unspoken boundaries about what topics are suitable for open discussion. Team members might feel comfortable discussing work mistakes or challenging each other's ideas, but hesitate to share something as personal as feelings of disconnection or loneliness. To address this challenge, we need to actively encourage conversations about connection and belonging.

OPENING UP THE CONVERSATION

Team members often take their cues about acceptable behaviour from their colleagues, especially from their managers or other leaders they regularly interact with. This is why it's useful for leaders to show that isolation in remote teams is a valid concern and that it's okay to bring up feelings of isolation – whether in team settings or with a manager individually.

Tim Burgess applies his belief in role modelling to various aspects of leadership. "What probably has the greatest impact is acknowledging it (loneliness) as a potential issue and being able to talk about it. So for me, that means modelling that behaviour. It's something that I always talk to people about. Here's my own personal experience, it's okay to talk about it."[5]

Team members will notice these efforts. You might remember Asia Hundley, a member of Tim's team, sharing her experience in Chapter 4 of grappling with the challenges of living abroad. She described how the initial excitement of a new place can mask feelings of disconnection, but as time passes, the reality of being away from family and friends sets in.

"I actually started thinking about it (feeling disconnected) because Tim – who's one of the founders of our company – would post articles in our company-wide chat about how to cope with working remotely and the different challenges you might face. When I would read those articles, I would start to think, 'Oh, maybe I haven't considered this. Maybe it is affecting me, and I just haven't realised it.'"

Tim's proactive sharing of articles about remote work challenges, including loneliness, helped spark reflection and discussion among employees like Asia, showing how simple actions by leaders can open up important conversations and encourage team members to reflect on their own experiences.

Marcus Wermuth also suggests it's important for leadership to set the tone for openness and vulnerability. He attributes much of his ability to address issues like disconnection to the example set by those above him in the organisation. "You, yourself, have to be vulnerable. That's something you have to work on yourself. I would say that my manager and the VP – even up to the CEO – their authenticity helped me in tapping more into this (learning to recognise the signs of loneliness and being open about these kinds of issues)."[6]

Marcus' experience highlights how a culture of openness and vulnerability can cascade through an organisation, from the CEO down to team managers, creating an environment where discussing feelings of disconnection becomes normalised and accepted. This foundation of psychological safety is further strengthened by inclusivity, where deliberate efforts are made to ensure all team members, regardless of their background or work situation, feel a sense of belonging and are treated equitably. It's important to note that some groups or individuals may, understandably, require added support, encouragement or time to build trust – particularly if they haven't historically felt safe within the workplace. This could apply to those from racial, religious, or sexual orientation and gender identity minority groups, individuals working in their second language, neurodivergent team members, parents returning to the workforce, or those with added caring responsibilities.

When employees feel included and valued, they are more likely to feel comfortable expressing any feelings of disconnection.

While psychological safety and vulnerability provide a foundation for meaningful connection, they shouldn't be our only focus. Rather than waiting for people to feel safe enough to open up about disconnection, we can proactively build connection through the ways we structure and organise our work.

CREATING STRUCTURE FOR CONNECTION

One of the most practical ways to foster connection is through clear systems for availability and communication laid down in a "team agreement". A team agreement is a collaborative document outlining how team members will communicate, collaborate, and conduct themselves to ensure they work effectively and harmoniously.

While this document will include high-level guidelines, it should also detail specific communication protocols, such as when team members are available for quick conversations or consultations. By establishing clear windows of availability, team members can make informed decisions about when to reach out, balancing the need for connection with respect for others' focus-time.

Setting expectations for active hours on communication platforms helps create a sense of presence and availability within a distributed team. Laurel Farrer used to do this with her team.

"We set the expectation that you are active on Slack for three to four hours a day, or you attend certain meetings, and there's the expectation articulated that you're engaged and vocal during the meetings. Hopefully, team members will always feel connected if they are participating in this 'checklist of engagement'."

By establishing these guidelines, ideally in agreement with team members, managers can provide a framework for connectivity and collaboration. In other words, the structure isn't there for the sake of it but, if adhered to properly, should act as a safety net for teams to experience a baseline level of connection no matter where they are logging on for the day.

Depending on the team's nature and maturity, it may be beneficial to agree on these protocols and formalise them in a team agreement. (Remember that remote teams need to deliberately create structures that co-located teams can often rely on emerging spontaneously.)

CONNECTING BEYOND THE TEAM

Just as communication within a team can be structured to foster connection, the same principles can be applied to building connections beyond the team.

Due to the nature of their work, managers can serve as connectors between their team and the broader organisation, creating pathways for information and relationship-building. By deliberately bringing insights, updates and context from other departments, managers can help their team members understand how their work fits into the larger organisational ecosystem and why certain decisions are made. This contextualisation can improve work quality and strengthens team members' sense of purpose and belonging to something larger than their immediate group.

Beyond information sharing, skilled managers actively cultivate their "introduction radar" – identifying valuable connection opportunities between their team members and colleagues elsewhere in the organisation. By facilitating these introductions with clear context about why the connection might be valuable, managers can help expand their team members' organisational networks and access to diverse perspectives. It's also worth encouraging them to take advantage of company-wide initiatives that can further strengthen these networks.

Developing an "introduction radar"

In remembering that connection at work can happen in a number of ways, you can see how these connections need not be purely professional. Personal circumstances and interests can also form the basis for meaningful workplace relationships beyond one's own team. Whether connecting new parents, colleagues with similar cultural backgrounds, or those who share hobbies or interests, these personal connections can lead to supportive relationships beyond the team – offering different perspectives and support in times of conflict.

As always, intentionality needs to be behind this strategy. Mapping your own connections across the organisation and regularly reviewing this network can help identify potential introductions that could benefit your team members' growth, influence, and sense of organisational connection – both professionally and personally.

This approach to networking can be turned into an exercise involving the whole team. Creating visual representations of key stakeholders, departments and individuals that a team regularly interacts with, including details about each relationship's purpose, frequency and quality can help team members realise the potential to identify new relationships and strengthen weak ties.

This visible reminder of a team's place within the broader organisational ecosystem can enhance members' sense of belonging and purpose, while providing practical pathways for accessing support and resources beyond the immediate team.

ROUTINELY CHECKING IN

While facilitating spontaneous interactions is valuable, many of our podcast guests emphasised the importance of structured, regular check-ins. For example, many teams in organisations like Buffer, use the "traffic light exercise" at the start of meetings. This involves team members indicating their current state using a simple colour code: green (feeling good), yellow (caution, might be stressed or tired), or red (struggling or facing significant challenges).

These check-ins don't necessarily have to happen in meetings – they can take place in asynchronous platforms, through dedicated channels. They can happen weekly, daily, or during challenging times or times of change.

The traffic light exercise serves multiple purposes. It allows the manager and team members to quickly gauge the emotional state of their colleagues, promoting empathy and understanding. It also provides a simple, non-intrusive way for employees to signal if they're facing difficulties, opening the door for support or intervention if needed. By normalising the sharing of non-positive states, you can create a culture where it's okay to not always be at 100%, reducing the pressure employees might feel to always present themselves as perfectly fine and in agreement with each other – something often referred to as "artificial harmony".

Sometimes a conversation is all it takes to address potential feelings of disconnection, but other times it might require rethinking how your team operates or communicates. To inspire you, here's a reminder of some of the actions Courtney Seiter has taken at an organisational level when she's seen people feel "yellow" or "red" after a traffic system exercise.

"When we hear some yellows and some reds, it can mean stress, and it can also mean isolation. So we point them to our existing resources, because sometimes they may not be aware of some of the stuff that's available to them. But every case is different, so there's always more we can do.

If it is an engineer who is feeling isolated, maybe we partner them with someone to do pair programming every day. Or maybe we can work with them to find some local organisations or meetups so they can go out in their city, wherever they might be in the world, and find some like-minded folks who have similar challenges.

Being a global organisation, the issue might be time zone specific. For example, we have a limited number of teammates in the Asia Pacific area. So when a few of them expressed feelings like, 'It's really quiet where we are, it's really hard to feel connected to the rest of the team', we tried a lot of different things to bring that section of the team more into the fold by going more asynchronous with a lot of our communication. It's hard to wake up and feel like you missed all the conversations and all the decisions have already been made. So, we moved more communication into an asynchronous format, slowed it down a little bit so folks could feel, rightly, like they were part of the process, as they absolutely should be.

It really just depends on what the situation is, where the isolation is coming from. But it's pretty safe to say that the key is to work with the teammates to find a solution. It's really important to go that extra mile to see if we can make that change."[7]

BUILDING THE BUSINESS CASE

While Buffer stands as a prime example of flexibility, we recognise that not all companies have values that guide the ongoing allocation of resources to adapt practices for their people's wellbeing and connection. As Tim Burgess told us in a comment on the first draft of this book: "Not all businesses are willing to change practices to accommodate a small number of their cohort. But the principle should be the same: work within your constraints and co-create a solution with the affected teammates."

Many managers genuinely believe that investing in connection is the right thing to do. The challenge often lies in justifying that investment to more senior leaders who are focused on immediate outputs. This is where data like that we shared in Chapter 4 can come in handy: 60% of remote workers cite connection to their organisation's mission or purpose as an influence in their intent to stay in their role; for hybrid it's 61% and for in-office workers, 55%.[8] These findings suggest that connection isn't a "nice to have" – it's a key driver of retention and engagement across all working arrangements.[9]

RESTRUCTURING THE WORK FOR CONNECTION

When addressing connection in remote teams, managers often find themselves navigating two related elements: the structure of work itself, and the patterns of communication that emerge from it. Redesigning teamwork can create opportunities for meaningful connection – from rotating team members across projects to foster cross-pollination of ideas, to implementing pair-working systems that enable colleagues to tackle complex problems together. As well as combating isolation, these approaches can create purposeful collaboration that enhances both individual growth and team capability.

Marcus Wermuth sees team connection not just as a cultural ideal, but as a practical foundation for better collaboration and performance. When he became manager of the Mobile Team at Buffer, Marcus decided to take a bird's-eye-view of how team members were working together. Initially, the company's iOS and

Android teams were separate, which reinforced a divide between them. To tackle this, he:

1. United the teams by emphasising their shared work, despite slight differences in platform.
2. Encouraged direct communication between team members, regardless of their specific role.
3. Visualised the team structure as a network rather than a traditional hierarchical organisational chart.

This approach helped to create a more interconnected team structure, without adding any extra workload or social activities. What Marcus intuitively understood was that connection at work happens in multiple dimensions.

THE 3 A'S OF CONNECTION

People connect at work in a range of ways, not just over purely social chats. As the practice of remote work continued post-pandemic and the risk of loneliness in remote teams started getting more attention, Pilar noticed that most of the advice on how to help remote workers socialise centred around organising social gatherings. While this is the most obvious way of addressing that we are social animals, we know that socialisation also happens as people work through tasks together, or when they interact through other work-focused activities.

Being a fan of creating frameworks that help people think through a challenge, Pilar created the 3 A's of Connection model. She suggests that people connect in three ways:

ACROSS the work: project meetings, working on tasks together, coordinating the work.

AROUND the work: talking about what is going on in the rest of the organisation, sharing articles, talking about the industry, attending work events.

AWAY from the work: talking about the weekend, sharing personal challenges, attending social activities.

When thinking of addressing connection, many teams and organisations assume that the connection people are missing is AWAY from the work. But what if people prefer to connect by working more closely on tasks and projects with colleagues, or having more opportunities for learning about what others do?

When thinking about connecting Across or Around the work, Pilar likes to think of "Visible Teamwork", the team-alternative to "Working Out Loud"[10]. On a practical level, Visible Teamwork refers mainly to asynchronous practices designed to make communication more flexible and decrease reliance on meetings.

For example, using project management tools that allow for visible task assignment can increase transparency and help team members understand how their work fits into the bigger picture. This sense of purpose and interconnectedness can significantly reduce feelings of isolation.

While the 3 A's can be addressed through additional interactions or activities, some of our most meaningful connection opportunities don't require additional activities or time away from work – they exist within our daily workflow. This is worth remembering particularly in high-pressure environments where dedicated connection time might seem impossible. By paying attention to how our routine interactions, communication patterns, and collaboration approaches either foster or hinder connection, we can make significant improvements without adding to already full calendars.

The 3 A's of connection

SPOTTING THE SIGNS OF DISCONNECTION

Setting up activities and protocols to help people stay connected is something managers are perfectly positioned to lead on. But it's just as important to make sure you have ways of spotting when someone begins to pull away. You want to be able to spot the signs that something is going wrong, before it starts to affect the work and the relationships in the team. This is something Marcus has noticed.

"With remote work, everything is results-oriented, so you might not notice something is wrong until the work or productivity is impacted. By the time you notice someone is less productive, it might not be too late, but it's already further along, meaning something has already happened. This is something to be aware of because it can happen easily – by the time you see a drop in productivity, the issue has progressed. So, while a results-oriented approach is effective, it can be tricky when dealing with these kinds of issues."

For managers who don't have daily face-to-face contact with their team members, monitoring engagement levels without being intrusive becomes something of an art form. As Laurel Farrer mentioned earlier, engagement guidelines can serve as a helpful tool to observe how team members participate in day-to-day conversations. This approach isn't about ensuring strict adherence to guidelines or micromanaging; rather, it's about being attuned to changes in behaviour.

If you notice a shift in someone's online behaviour, whether in asynchronous chats or during meetings, make a mental note. Should this change persist, it might be worth checking-in with them.

For instance, if a team member who typically shares witty GIFs in the #random channel daily suddenly goes silent for a week, or if someone who always updates their tasks on a progress board begins to fall behind, it could signal that something's amiss.

The goal isn't to enforce rigid rules, but to identify potential issues early and offer support if needed, all while respecting individual work styles and privacy. You can use the visible change in behaviour as a prompt to say, "You were really quiet during the stand-up meeting. Is there something going on?" Or, "Hey, what happened to the cat pictures you used to post so regularly?."

Establishing routines to help people feel connected, whether through visible teamwork practices or structured connection points, forms the foundation of a well-functioning remote team. But these systems alone aren't enough. Those people who need real time interactions to feel truly connected with their colleagues require a different set of tools and practices.

This leads us to the second chapter on the role of the manager, to discuss in more detail how meetings, one-on-ones, and regular check-ins can create a fully rounded approach to connection in remote teams.

SUMMARY

- Clear communication protocols, including active hours on communication platforms, help to ensure a sense of presence and availability.

- Regularly scheduled check-ins provide structure and opportunities to address potential issues early on.

- Managers should make note of shifts in communication patterns, such as decreased participation or changes in tone as this can indicate issues including growing disconnection.

- Proactive check-ins with team members using open-ended questions to encourage conversation.

- A mix of synchronous and asynchronous methods of communications can help capture input from the entire team.

- Restructuring work by visualising the team as a network rather than a hierarchy can foster deeper connection.

- The 3 A's of connection provide a variety of connection opportunities across the work, around the work, and away from work to cater to different preferences.

CONTINUING THE CONVERSATION

1. How can we, as individuals, role-model openness and vulnerability to create a more psychologically safe

environment for team members to discuss feelings of disconnection?

2. What can our team do to create structure for connection, such as establishing clear communication protocols?

3. What actions can our team take to address potential disconnection by adapting communication practices, restructuring work, and providing varied connection opportunities?

7

MANAGER SUPPORT: BUILDING CONNECTION IN REAL TIME

While asynchronous communication and visible teamwork practices form the foundation of remote team collaboration, regular meetings also play a vital role in fostering connection for many workers. Some people simply need real time interaction to feel engaged with their colleagues and part of a team. The key is finding the right balance, as meeting needs vary significantly between individuals. Some team members may thrive with just a weekly, casual check-in, while others benefit from decision-making meetings to feel connected and aligned with their teammates. Understanding and accommodating these different preferences helps ensure everyone can work effectively.

In this chapter, we cover the role of meetings in helping team members feel connected, the practice of one-on-ones in maintaining individual relationships, and finally, why managers need their own support systems to effectively lead remote teams.

TEAM MEETINGS

Meetings have a bad name. Let's rephrase that: useless meetings have a bad name. They're often referred to as time-wasters, where nothing gets done and they get in the way of people getting on with "the real work".

But, especially in remote teams, meetings can provide important points of connection and socialisation. This socialising can happen in different ways: during work planning sessions, when exploring challenging projects, and in the more obvious social chats when talking about a popular book, or home-renovation challenges. Even those people like Pilar, who swear by asynchronous communication as the key to making remote work sustainable, can see the benefits of gathering online with collaborators and team members. Laughter and warmth spread faster in real time.

Laughter spreads faster in real time

Dr. Richard MacKinnon explains why these moments of connection aren't a distraction from work, but an essential part of what makes team thrive: "If you see social contact in the workplace as detracting from productivity, you're looking at it as a kind of a zero sum game, and it doesn't work that way at all. These interactions contribute to team effectiveness, and they contribute to team trust and psychological safety. It means that people are more willing to do things that are helpful to them when there are levels of trust and familiarity."[1]

While asynchronous communication makes our schedules more flexible, it can also lead to misunderstandings or delays in decision-making. Meetings allow for instant clarification, quick idea-generation, and the sharing of emotion which can be difficult to replicate in text-based formats.

Meetings can also serve as a structured time for collective problem-solving and decision-making, giving team members a real-time, shared goal to work towards. This sense of shared purpose can combat feelings of isolation by reinforcing that each individual is part of a larger team working together. It can reinforce their value to the team, and provide the mental stimulation that, if lacking, might contribute to loneliness.

Furthermore, meetings can offer visibility into the broader context of work and the challenges faced by others. Many of us often share information spontaneously in meetings that we might not think to share during our asynchronous interactions – either because the thought doesn't occur to us, or because we don't want to commit that information to writing. This visibility can help combat the "information isolation" that Laurel Farrer often mentions.

Marcus Wermuth shares a similar perspective on "information isolation". He says that, even in transparent companies, it's easy to lose track of what's happening or to miss important updates. As an engineer, he experienced this firsthand, struggling to stay connected with the broader organisation. "Even though the company is transparent, sometimes you just lose track of things, or things don't get forwarded to you and you don't see them."

Combatting information isolation doesn't have to be a difficult task. One option is to create space for non-task-related information in regular meetings. You might allocate a few minutes at the beginning of each meeting for team members to share personal updates or interesting experiences, or incorporate a brief "round robin" segment where each participant shares one piece of information unrelated to current tasks, such as an industry insight or a useful tool they've discovered.

As a manager or individual contributor, you can role model this behaviour by occasionally sharing broader company updates or insights that might not directly relate to the meeting's agenda but contribute to your team's overall understanding and connection. These practices can help combat information isolation and foster a more connected team culture within your existing meeting structure.

From a manager's perspective, the key is to balance the different kinds of meetings that fulfil various operational and connection needs, while ensuring they are balanced with asynchronous communication, which for some might continue to provide the best point of connection.

Marcus suggests allowing flexibility in meeting frequency and duration. While some team members might prefer "a one-on-one call with another engineer, but only every two weeks, or only when there's stuff on the agenda, some individuals might need ad-hoc one-on-one meetings to develop strong relationships, rather than always experiencing the group dynamics prevalent in whole team meetings."

Despite all these benefits, let's remember that meeting quality matters more than quantity. The key is finding the right balance for your team, ensuring that meetings serve their purpose of connection and collaboration without becoming burdensome.

NOT HYBRID MEETINGS, BUT ONLINE MEETINGS

While we initially set out to focus on remote teams rather than hybrid work arrangements – which could fill several chapters on their own – we wanted to touch briefly on hybrid meetings here, as they've become increasingly common.

Unless a meeting is run extremely well, or a team has refined their meeting practices, having some people gathered in a meeting room while others attend online intensifies the feelings of disconnection.

Those joining virtually often struggle to participate fully, feeling like observers rather than active participants. Meanwhile, people in the room may be at a disadvantage if they don't have easy access to chat and other online tools.

One way to address this imbalance is to have everyone join from their own device, enabling participants to gain equal presence.

Hybrid

Online

Each person appears in their own video window, can unmute themselves to speak, and experiences the same meeting dynamics as their colleagues. This approach prevents an "us vs. them" dynamic from developing between office-based and remote staff, helping maintain team cohesion.

ONE-ON-ONES

We've seen how managers can role-model openness about the challenges of disconnection and design team interactions to foster stronger connections. Now, let's turn to an important management activity: one-on-ones. These individual conversations provide a unique opportunity to support team members' wellbeing and use your insight into the team's work to address disconnection on a personal level. Those moments, when you're on your own with one of your team members, give you a chance to show them they matter.

These types of conversations will come more easily with some team members: maybe those you spend more time with, or those who regularly express their thoughts in public (in writing, or in meetings), or simply those with whom you have more in common.

After all, you are human too.

But it might be those people with whom it doesn't come easy to converse with who need it the most. It's worth raising your self-awareness about your levels of comfort in these situations. Are there times when you shy away from showing interest, or having meaningful conversations with some of your team members? Are you missing out on an opportunity with some of your team members to get to know them just that little bit better?

Regular one-on-ones become even more important if you have team members in different time zones who might find it challenging to reach out spontaneously. In cases where it doesn't come as naturally, it can be helpful to have a plan or structure to fall back on.

Structuring your one-on-ones

In remote teams, managers need to develop an extra "radar" to detect changes in a person's rhythm, language, communication style, and work patterns. Similar to setting communication protocols and regular check-ins at a team level, structured one-on-ones can help you identify changes in a team member's behaviour.

Don't shy away from planning your questions. A framework allows for both structure and spontaneity. Alongside those questions you might ask about their work, try to incorporate questions that might give you a clue that someone is beginning to feel like they're drifting away from the team. Furthermore, as Tim Burgess noted, asking a question on a regular basis also means you get a baseline for their "normal" response and can better recognise if something changes.[2]

You could ask questions like the following:

- Have there been times when it's been difficult to reach me or others when you needed us?
- Is work interfering with your life outside of work?
- Are there any discussions you feel you should be part of but aren't?
- What could we do to help you feel more connected to the team or organisation?

Tim also suggests asking questions even before noticing a team member is withdrawing. "You can also ask people, 'Is there anything I should look out for as a sign you might be feeling disconnected?' followed by, 'What would you like me to do if I see this happening?'"

While some of these are closed questions, they can open up important conversations. Consider sending them in advance or using follow-up prompts like, "Take your time to think over the last few weeks."

This doesn't mean there's no value in having unplanned

conversations in your one-on-one. On the contrary, changing the format or having an agenda-less conversation can prompt individuals to raise issues they might have thought are not relevant to these one-on-ones.

Many managers even prompt their team members to set their own agenda for their one on ones, either on an ad-hoc basis or regularly, under the understanding that this is "their meeting." While this practice may make it more challenging at times to address topics like disconnection, it does make these conversations more likely to be led by the team member.

The personal touch

Remembering personal details shared by team members, whether in casual chats or during meetings, can be powerful. It shows you care about them as individuals, not just colleagues. Make notes if needed – it's not calculated, but thoughtful.

These personal insights can help you detect changes that might impact their sense of social connection. For instance, if a team member mentions taking up a new hobby but later drops it due to work, it could flag potential issues with work-life balance or social interaction.

By combining structured questions with a personal touch in your one-on-ones, you create a space where team members feel valued and comfortable discussing any feelings of disconnection. This approach complements the open culture you're fostering at the team level, ensuring that every individual has the opportunity to connect and be heard.

IT GETS LONELY AT THE TOP

This might well feel like a cliché, but it can get lonely at the top. While we have been suggesting transparency as one of the antidotes to disconnection at work, the nature of team leadership often requires making difficult decisions and handling sensitive information that can't always be shared with team members. This discretion can create an emotional distance which can leave managers feeling disconnected from the team, and even lonely.

Managers and leaders are still people, exposed to the same challenges as everyone else. In addition to this, leadership often comes with its own unique form of solitude. This is not something we covered during the Connection and Disconnection series, but it's something that Pilar and Tim picked up a few years later, while recording for their podcast Management Café.

In an episode called The Loneliness of Leading, Tim said, "There's a degree of separation that comes when you're put into the position of leading the team. You're contributing, but you're contributing in different ways. It's a different dynamic."[3] This separation manifests in various ways, from the inability to share certain information with team members, to the weight of sole decision-making responsibility. Furthermore, managers must be careful about how much personal information or struggles to share with their team members, as sometimes the unbalanced power dynamics can put the team member in an awkward position.

The first step in avoiding loneliness is to develop a high degree of self-awareness about what you need as a leader, and engage in regular reflection. Marcus Wermuth learned this early on in his career.

"I learned – especially during my career shift from engineer to manager – that self-reflection or self-awareness is a huge thing and it's something that brings you forward a tonne. When it comes to the loneliness problem or other problems with myself, I ask myself a load of questions. Sometimes I relate it back to having an engineering background. Although I don't code anymore, I still tend to ask a lot of questions around feelings: 'Why is that? Why is it working like that?'"

Once you understand what can affect your feelings of connection, you might find it useful to have a support system around you. One way to find this, especially if you work in a large organisation, is to deliberately network within the company to find others with similar responsibilities to yours. That's why it's worth spending time scanning internal social networks and even external ones to find potential "buddies." Another option is to utilise development opportunities and attend training events, conferences or meet-ups to connect with other managers.

Building your network outside of your organisation can provide valuable perspectives, emotional support, and professional growth opportunities that may not be available internally. These online communities have been particularly valuable to Tim, who found the relationships more positive and rewarding than he expected. Moving away from his initial perception of business networks as transactional "old boys networks" focused on job hunting, Tim discovered the value of building genuine connections based on mutual interests and a desire to be helpful.

You can build your network through professional associations, leadership forums, or online communities. The beauty of the online world is that you can connect with people from all walks of life, regardless of where you're based. This is a great opportunity to leverage your skills as a remote worker, which include building relationships at a distance.

LET'S GET PRACTICAL

While we've presented a wide range of strategies for managers to foster connection and prevent isolation, implementing everything at once isn't necessary, or even recommended.

You can think of these last two chapters as a menu of options, from which you can choose what best suits your team's needs and your organisational context. Instead of feeling pressured to implement everything, start by identifying the most pressing needs in your team, or pick a strategy that you might find easy to try out, or one you might enjoy.

We'd also recommend that you work with your team to select one or two strategies that seem most relevant to their work and their needs. By modelling a thoughtful and considered approach, you can show that it's okay to take things slowly – and we know how rare that is these days. Once you and your team are comfortable with those strategies, you can gradually add more as needed. Adopting this phased approach can ensure that your efforts to address isolation do not themselves become a source of stress or burnout.

There is also a chance that some of your team members may be resistant to the kind of initiatives helping people to "connect". While some might feel overwhelmed by additional meetings or social interactions, others may question the value of such activities, especially if they seem contrived. It's not uncommon for individuals to hesitate to participate in something designed to strengthen relationships at work. This could be based on their working style preferences, or on disappointing experiences with similar initiatives in the past. Team members might be concerned about adding more work, however meaningful, to an already packed schedule.

If you notice resistance, acknowledge these valid concerns and introduce flexible, opt-in connection opportunities that respect both time and personal preferences. You might create varied touch points throughout the working week, from brief virtual coffee breaks to more structured team discussions, allowing your team to engage at their comfort level. Focus on fostering an environment where connection feels natural and valuable rather than forced.

Above all, lead by example and keep track of what's working. If an activity hasn't gained traction, acknowledge this openly, end the experiment and discuss what you've all learned about team dynamics. When something does work – especially if people mention feeling happier or more productive – celebrate it and analyse why it resonates with your team. Set regular review points, as needs and contexts change over time.

As time passes, everyone on your team will face different challenges and changes in their lives that affect how they experience remote work. Their sense of connection – or disconnection – is personal, and what works for them may shift over time. Your role is to listen carefully, understand what they need, and support them in finding their own balance. This might involve adjusting how they interact with colleagues, or finding ways of building connections outside of work.

And speaking of individual needs – whether you're a manager or not, you'll have your own relationship with remote work to consider. To help you with this, the next chapter looks at how individuals can maintain their own sense of connection, regardless of their position in an organisation.

SUMMARY

- Well-structured meetings provide connection and socialisation opportunities. Meetings offer real-time clarification, idea generation, and shared laughter, which can be difficult to replicate in asynchronous communication.
- One-on-ones show team members that they matter, especially those who might be harder to connect with.
- Planned questions uncover potential feelings of disconnection, while also allowing for spontaneous conversations.
- Developing self-awareness about personal needs for connection and engaging in regular reflection is essential for managers.
- Managers should build support networks both within and outside the organisation to gain valuable perspectives and emotional support.

CONTINUING THE CONVERSATION

1. Do our meetings offer visibility into the broader context of work and the challenges faced by others?

2. How can I/we structure our one-on-ones to ensure feelings of connection and/or spot the signs of loneliness early on?

3. How can I cultivate my own support systems to avoid loneliness and effectively lead my team?

THE ROLE OF THE INDIVIDUAL

W hile the set environment of a workplace - including its culture, policies, values and resources - will always play a significant role in how connected team members feel (whether they are remote or otherwise) there will also be many areas individuals can impact.

In this chapter, we'll share some personal strategies anyone can implement, no matter where they sit in the organisational structure. And, while we think they work best in conjunction with strategies and initiatives implemented by the organisation and management, they'll be useful even if you find yourself in an unsupportive environment.

But before we look at what actions we can take as individuals, let's remember the importance of self-awareness.

UNDERSTANDING THE SELF

Unlike a physical ailment, feeling isolated, lonely or disconnected isn't always outwardly visible to others – or truthfully even to ourselves.

While an individual may eventually show signs of struggle such as turning in a piece of work late, missing a meeting or withdrawing in collaboration sessions, these signs tend to present later down the line, and for those who are well-versed in masking how they feel, they may not come at all.

With this in mind, it can be very difficult for even the most well-intentioned manager, HR representative or colleague to identify disconnection just by observation alone.

This means that, in order to detect and flag feelings of isolation or disconnection, it has to be up to the individual to notice these feelings and choose whether or not to act on them. This often requires at least some level of self-reflection, which is especially important for remote workers who don't always have a lot of incidental or 'forced' changes of environment, or in-built interactions with people.

In contrast, when you work in an office environment, you often have some down time built into your commute where your mind can wander. Whether it be waiting for the bus, sitting in traffic, or walking from the station, these moments are important for processing and evaluating how we are feeling. Once we get to the office there are other in-built moments of movement and interaction that can break up the day including moving between meeting rooms or grabbing lunch outside. For remote workers, especially those working from the same place every day, these moments are largely absent.

To quote Laurel Farrer, "Sometimes our days and our lives blur together in remote work and our environments aren't changing as much, and so therefore it's hard to identify why we feel bad."[1]

LAYING THE GROUNDWORK FOR SELF-AWARENESS

For many people, self-reflection is easier said than done. It's a skill that doesn't always come naturally and can require external support. But, like most things in life, it's something that can be developed over time, and is incredibly rewarding with countless applications.

As a workplace psychologist, Dr. Richard MacKinnon has plenty of experience supporting people towards this goal.

"We can learn to be more self-aware. If we couldn't, I wouldn't have a job. Fundamentally, a lot of the development work I do with people is helping them to notice more about themselves so that they can notice more about others," he said in our episode on individual contributions to connection.

Dr. MacKinnon often takes on the role of asking the questions which facilitate this kind of reflective thinking for those who may find it difficult to do on their own. It's not necessarily his role to provide answers, but to guide his clients to find solutions for themselves.

"To me, coaching is all about questions. Does that work for you, or are you missing something here? And if you are missing something, what could you do about it? And hopefully they will come up with the idea," Dr. MacKinnon said.

For those who don't have access to a workplace psychologist or coach, but could use the external prompt, it may be useful to seek out a mentor, online forum or group. Some employers would support this as a form of career development, and by asking for this it may help implement a new policy for the rest of your team.

Whether you have this kind of external support or not, there are practical steps you can take to raise your self-awareness and understand your context. Alongside sharing context and advice during our podcast season, our guests also offered personal strategies that helped them feel less isolated. Drawing from those insights, and our own experiences, we've outlined a practical approach that might be useful.

Step one: checking-in

In the same way that we all have different ways of thinking, learning and problem-solving, there are many methods of reflection. Some love to journal, others love talk-therapy, some enjoy prompts, others uninterrupted flow of consciousness. Some might need creative outlets like art or drawing to understand what they're feeling, others need movement like running or yoga. It might be the stillness of nature that helps some, while others would prefer to work out their problem in a physical way by organising a messy drawer or sorting out an unruly garden.

No method is wrong, the priority is finding something that works for you and being open to other methods as our needs change.

However, by using questions, as Dr. MacKinnon suggests, we are able to approach our problems with curiosity instead of judgement, and the solutions we come up with tend to be more personal and unique to our actual situation.

Step two: recording data

Asking questions is only the first step – capturing and tracking your answers is equally important. By gathering this data, we're able to reflect on progress and change over time.

In what we've called the slow creep, what we can handle in the first few months of working from home might be different six months to a year later, which might be different again a few years after that. Without somehow tracking these changes over time, it can be difficult to stay on top of them as the changes are often gradual.

When Bree first started working remotely, she was living in an apartment with incredible natural light. It was summer in Australia and the sun rose early, and she would wake up without an alarm each morning. She had a peaceful morning routine in place, and found her new role interesting and engaging. She didn't feel like she had to try very hard to start her work feeling motivated because she was really dialled into the work and her team.

Later that year, Bree moved to Canada where her environment completely changed. She was waking up in the dark, living with another family who had much more lively morning habits, and her team was now in an entirely different time zone. What worked in Australia, wasn't working anymore.

At first this was difficult to wrap her head around. Having to implement new habits to muster up the engagement that initially felt inherent was disorientating and difficult to stick with. However, mulling over what had changed and what aspects of her earlier routine she was craving helped her to identify possible solutions that ended up supporting the transition.

Bree's journaling practice was helpful here. While she wasn't writing out specific questions and answers, her daily stream of consciousness pages (something she picked up from Julia Cameron's *The Artist's Way*[2]) revealed certain themes over time.

If a blank page is daunting there are also guided journals, online prompts, apps, programmes and specific exercise handbooks that can all help facilitate this kind of ongoing practice.

Step three: experimenting

Once you've identified that you may be feeling disconnected, it's time to trial some solutions. This might look like speaking to your manager, or utilising one of your company's wellbeing programmes. Perhaps you need to be better at logging off in the evenings so you sign up for a class or make some regular plans with friends. You might be feeling disconnected from your work and seek out a mentor or take on a new project that reignites your interest.

Remember, it's not about the specifics. Rather, it's about going through the process of finding out what you need to thrive, and implementing it into your routine. And sometimes that takes experimenting.

As Laurel said: "I've been a remote worker for 13 years now, and what worked for me in the beginning is very different than what worked for me five years ago, which is very different than what works for me now. So always be evaluating yourself. Just like a manager evaluates you professionally, evaluate yourself as a worker and as a human being and say, 'what do I need to thrive? And how can I fill that gap?'"

TAKING INDIVIDUAL ACTION

Just like the methods of reflecting and recording progress can and should differ person-to-person, the routines that help individuals feel connected will also be different.

Taking care of yourself

The area individuals often have the most control over, whatever position they hold in a company, is their own routines and habits *outside* of the workplace.

Without the external pressure of having to leave on time for their commute, remote workers can struggle (at least sometimes) to stick to healthy morning routines such as getting dressed everyday, eating breakfast or exercising. It can also be tempting to skip a proper lunch break or take time away from the computer throughout the day, as there's no need to walk to the sandwich shop down the street or make your way to the train for your commute home. Additionally, it can be harder to switch off at the end of the day without the natural influence of others packing up around you.

Mandating in-office work isn't the answer here. The inflexibility of compulsory work hours can also promote unhealthy routines. Having to be in-office at a certain time each day can mean you have to choose between getting enough sleep or making breakfast, and long commutes can cut into time you'd otherwise use for exercise.

Taking care of ourselves is fundamental to being able to give our best throughout the work day. A lack of routine over time can leave us feeling exhausted, unprepared and overwhelmed – not exactly in the best place to be productive, let alone connect with those around us.

Designing your work day

For some remote workers, structuring their days isn't a problem. There's more than enough work and scheduled meetings to keep them busy and on task throughout the day, and errands like putting on a load of washing or cooking lunch at home provide enough breaks to keep momentum flowing throughout the day.

For others, perhaps those whose work is naturally more isolated by task or time zone, it may be useful to implement structures that simulate the external pressures that exist inherently in the office.

Many remote workers like to do something similar each morning to simulate a sort of "commute" and get them in the headspace to work. This might be a morning dog walk or listening to a specific podcast while getting ready for the day.

Bree does pilates classes a couple mornings a week. She finds the momentum carries her throughout the rest of her day, making her feel on task and connected to her work. With more time on the other days, she doesn't have to move as quickly to get ready for the day and funnily enough, it's these days she'll find herself running late or not feeling as motivated to get started.

Some people might need to go as far as diarising their social interactions, whether work-related or not. Otherwise they might never happen.

Getting out of the house

Some remote workers find working from their homes particularly isolating. In our podcast season, Asia Hundley shared how switching up her routine and working from a co-working space completely changed how isolated she was feeling, even though she was technically still remote from her team.

"I think getting out, not being physically isolated, and then also getting into a routine of waking up in the morning, and getting dressed and going to the office, so to speak, really helped."[3]

Bree has been a long-term lover of working from coffee shops and libraries. She finds the intentionality of going somewhere to work incredibly motivating, and the small interactions with people in her community really help fend off any feelings of isolation.

But it doesn't have to be this significant. While you may not have a commute in your routine forcing you out of the house, remote work can often afford individuals the flexibility to incorporate errands into their day. Simple tasks, like hanging the washing or picking up a package from the post office, can provide healthy breaks in between work tasks that feel personally productive, and provide an opportunity to get outside.

The value of positive social interactions

While many of our routines and rituals are about taking care of ourselves, a lot of them also provide us opportunities for social interactions, such as a morning walk, going to a café or attending exercise classes.

We know instinctively (and through social research) that having meaningful relationships affects our wellbeing. But there is also evidence that "social interactions with the more peripheral members of our social networks contribute to our wellbeing".[4] These "weak ties" can include casual conversations with colleagues at work, but are not limited to the workplace. They could be brief exchanges at the cafe counter, or, in Pilar's case, waving at the waiters of her favourite local Indian restaurant.

When we're already feeling isolated, we're more inclined to shy away from these kinds of interactions, but making an effort to say hello to neighbours as you pass them on a walk, or interacting with people at a local store or class can help us feel connected to our community, and more positive in general. It all adds up.

We can replicate these interactions virtually, too. When Bree worked for a company with a large international team, one of her colleagues would start every day with a good morning message in a group chat she had set up with everyone in the region. These messages provided an initial connection point, but they also provided opportunities for further interaction later on. Bree saw first hand how a 'Happy Taco Tuesday' message led to sharing recipes and photos from someone making Mexican food later in the day.

Chat-based collaboration platforms are a common place to connect with colleagues over non-work related topics. You'd be hard pressed to find a functioning Slack workspace without a #Music channel, and it's easy to see the merits of a #Book-club or #Pets channel where colleagues can share photos, updates and recommendations. If you have an interest in something, chances are there's someone else that would like to know about it, so creating a Slack channel is a low-risk place to start.

A colleague of Bree's in a previous job set up irregular "co-work meetings" which had a group of colleagues meet over Zoom not for agenda-based meetings, but to work alongside each other like they would in an office environment.

Pilar also went through a phase of using an online co-working space when she fancied bumping into someone for a quick chat. The Virtual Team Talk community had a space in the virtual office Sococo, accessible to all members throughout the day. Every now and then, Pilar would drop in to see who was around and have a quick chat with them, often just over instant message. These interactions brightened her day, and helped her get to know some community members better.

Similarly for Dr. MacKinnon, finding someone he could regularly have video calls with helped him to feel less alone throughout the work day.

"I realised that [by] just opening Skype and having a quick chat with someone in a similar circumstance, [it] went a long way in the working day for me. And it didn't have to be anything deep or long, it didn't require me to derail my day for that kind of social contact."

Supporting others

Sometimes it's the intention behind these social interactions that makes the difference. Dr. Holt-Lunstad suggests that reaching out and supporting others can actually have stronger benefits to us than if we receive that support ourselves. Helping people makes us feel like a necessary player, and gives us a sense of purpose and a common goal that we can all work towards.

"For those who might be feeling like they might be a bit isolated, or feeling awkward in a social situation, if they can look around the room and see who might need someone to talk to, and think of it as a way to help someone else – it's a way to feel less vulnerable, and a way to potentially get ourselves out of that situation and help others in the process."[5]

Supporting others

Teresa Douglas, who shared her experience role-modelling vulnerability in Chapter 6, also emphasises that reaching out doesn't have to be a grand gesture — and it doesn't always come naturally. Especially in remote settings, she sees it as a skill we can learn and practice, just like any other.

"I'm shameless on Slack and email. If I've been at a meeting with somebody and I thought they said something good, or if there's something I didn't quite understand, or I wanted clarity, it's an excuse to reach out and say, 'Hey, do you mind if I have ten minutes of your time? Just to get a little more on that thing you said in the meeting? Because that was interesting'. People usually give you ten minutes."[6]

Teresa's point brings to mind Pilar's 3 A's framework. It's not always necessary to make specific plans "away" from the work. Sometimes our day-to-day activities with our co-workers and managers provide the necessary opportunities to connect. Sometimes we don't need to do anything extra but pay attention to how we are communicating "across" and "around" the work.

Engaging with the work

In a similar way, positive work interactions are also incredibly impactful. While these may seem less in our control, as they rely on a few more moving parts than a wave to a neighbour, there are still some areas individuals can have an effect on – namely their own efforts.

As simple as it sounds, being an active participant in your meetings, projects, presentations and the like will help you feel connected to your work. You may not feel excited by every task on your list, and if you're already feeling isolated from your team it may be tempting to disengage further, but actively speaking up in meetings, sharing your ideas freely, coming prepared with solutions and examples when noticing problems makes a difference.

To initiate this process, it might be helpful to identify the things you like best about your work, and spot the opportunities where you can do more of them.

When you put in effort, even in a project no one else will see, you are showing yourself that you think the work is worthwhile. These intentional efforts, however small, strengthen your bonds to your work, because you have to really focus your attention and be present. These practices reiterate and signal to yourself that it's something that's important to you, and with time, your feelings of connection will often catch up.

. . .

Maximising workplace benefits

Something similar could be said about wellness programmes or social initiatives, which research shows are relatively low-attended.

The 2024 article, "Employees Not Participating in Wellness Programs", reported a significant disconnect between programme availability and employee utilisation. The article cited a survey of over 900 employers and employees, where most employers (86.2%) said they offered health and wellness programmes, but also reported struggling with low participation.

The findings cited the major barriers to participation as lack of time (60.9%) and a limited interest in offerings (36.9%), but also a lack of awareness and access (34.2%), which suggests at least some level of communication breakdown between the organisation and its workforce.[7]

Despite the disconnected realities these statistics point to, if your organisation is one of the many that has invested in setting up wellness programmes, this is certainly something that is worth seeking out.

As we mentioned in Chapter 5, in one of Bree's recent remote roles, the company offered a subscription to the Calm app. While meditation wasn't something she'd previously made much time for, she downloaded the app early on with good intentions. Over a year went by before she finally did a 10-minute guided meditation in the middle of a particularly stressful work day, and it was something that quickly became a lifeline throughout a difficult project.

While your organisation's programmes may not seem to be exactly in line with your interests, sometimes it's worth trying something out of the ordinary as you never know how it might help. It's also worth reaching out to your HR team or manager, as there may be something on offer you weren't aware of or an opportunity to integrate a new service.

. . .

Seeking professional help

While we've laid out a number of strategies around self-reflection, routines, and building connections, we need to acknowledge that some people may need additional support once they notice they're unwell. Even after following the above steps, you could still be feeling overwhelmed. If this is the case, remember that professional support is available through doctors, therapists, or psychologists. Sometimes we can get bombarded by all kinds of solutions that work for others and think that there's some kind of quick fix out there for us if we just keep looking – when actually there might be some serious underlying issues.

This is where well-intentioned suggestions to call a friend or start a hobby can really fall short, when what we really need is professional support. Marcus Wermuth regularly writes on his blog about his ongoing use of therapy as a resource to understand and better himself. He's passionate about destigmatising the process and often will talk about his experiences within his team in the hopes that leading by example might encourage others to get help if they need it.

"We all go to see a doctor if our knee hurts, or if our finger hurts. But going to a therapist always seems like, 'Oh my God, what is going on?' But it's just a different type of doctor to fix a problem. That's how I see it."

Rather than providing a universal solution to disconnection, we hope this chapter has opened up possibilities for creating connections that align with your context and situation.

We're not specifically pushing for walks or co-working spaces or sending emoji filled messages to your workmates. What we are suggesting is prioritising listening, reflecting, and questioning. We're advocating for trying something new and noticing whether it was enriching or exhausting, committing to practices you know you love and are helpful to you, and treating yourself with kindness on the days when you struggle to get by. While you're at it, reach out to people you work with in whatever ways you can, and when it all gets too much, know that it's more than okay to ask for help.

SUMMARY

- Self-reflection helps identify potential issues early on and allows individuals to develop tailored solutions.

- Establishing daily routines and structuring your workday are important for overall wellbeing and work productivity.

- You can simulate the external pressures of an office environment by working from co-working spaces, setting up virtual co-work meetings, or scheduling regular video calls with colleagues.

- Engaging in positive social interactions, however brief, adds up.

- Specific routines and solutions will vary for each individual. Experimentation is a key factor in finding what works best.

- Seek professional help when needed. If isolation becomes overwhelming, consider speaking to a doctor or therapist for support.

CONTINUING THE CONVERSATION

1. What specific practices can I adopt to better understand my connection needs and identify potential issues early on?

2. In what ways can I leverage my work environment to foster connection, such as by working from co-working spaces,

setting up virtual co-work meetings, or scheduling regular video calls with colleagues?

3. How can I build my support network at work by identifying colleagues who can provide emotional support and guidance through work-related challenges?

4. What resources are available in the organisation to support my mental health and wellbeing?

THE FUTURE OF CONNECTION IN REMOTE TEAMS

A s we've seen in the last four chapters, technology can play a vital role in not just productivity, but also in helping people develop relationships at work. Collaboration tools and meeting platforms were already widespread when we recorded the "Connection and Disconnection in Remote Teams" season, but the adoption of emerging technologies has taken huge leaps forward since then.

The explosion of generative AI in 2022 introduced new dimensions in the conversation about loneliness and its impact in the workplace, including team dynamics. This means we can't publish a book on loneliness in 2025 without "delving into the new world of generative AI", and exploring how new technologies (chatbots in particular) can affect relationships at work.

NEW TECHNOLOGIES: FUTURE THREATS TO CONNECTION, OR POSSIBLE ANSWERS TO LONELINESS?

Throughout this book, we've hailed technology as the great enabler of connection in remote teams, from video conferencing to collaborative documents and asynchronous communication platforms. Beyond simply using these tools, for many remote workers – especially those who've chosen this way of working – experimenting with technology becomes part of their professional identity and team culture.

As technology evolves, and there are more new shiny things to play with, the very process of experimenting with new tools can itself become a connecting experience. When colleagues test new software, share feedback, or troubleshoot technical issues together, they create shared experiences and even inside jokes that strengthen their relationships as they connect "around the work" (one of our three "A's of connection").

New technologies aren't always as promising as they're held out to be though, as is the case with virtual reality headsets. Virtual reality (VR) platforms (which are typically accessed through headsets) allow people to gather in shared virtual spaces, where individuals appear as avatars, sometimes very much like their real selves. Users can move around, gesture, and interact with virtual objects and whiteboards. For some individuals, this can provide a stronger sense of spatial presence compared to traditional video calls, and this greater sense of physical closeness can result in feeling more emotionally connected too.

At the time of writing, however, the platforms still experience glitches, and the headsets themselves can be physically isolating from one's immediate environment, as well as creating a sense of "fake" that can leave people longing to be together in a physical room without wearing cumbersome headgear.

These kinds of immersive and spatial computing promise to recreate the rich non-verbal cues of face-to-face interactions in virtual environments. Ambient computing (technology embedded in our environment that reacts to contextual cues) and IoT-driven experiences (interconnected smart devices that personalise interactions through data sharing) could further personalise shared online workspaces.

Although this tech can lead to some positive experiences, much of it is geared at trying to replicate connection in the physical space, instead of looking for new ways of connecting online. As we've seen throughout this book, the most effective approaches to fostering connection acknowledge and accommodate diverse personal preferences and needs. But this does not mean we need to rush into trying out all those new technologies as soon as they are available. While experimentation can be valuable, we must remain focused on how these tools genuinely serve our need for meaningful connection rather than chasing technological novelty for its own sake.

However, some technological advances are difficult to ignore. At the time of writing, it's obvious that Large Language Models (LLMs) and their chatbot interfaces go beyond mere trend or fad. They are already reshaping how knowledge workers think, work, and connect – with both promising and concerning implications for team relationships.

NEW TECH, NEW TEAM MEMBER?

Large Language Models (LLMs) are advanced artificial intelligence systems trained on vast amounts of text data, enabling them to generate human-like responses to written prompts. Their chatbots - interfaces powered by these models like Claude AI or ChatGPT – can simulate conversation, answer questions, and assist with tasks ranging from writing to coding.

For the seasoned remote worker (who doesn't spend all day in meetings and works independently most of the time), these chatbots can become the first point of call when they get stuck, have a question or need feedback. These chatbots can feel like always-on collaborators – generating ideas, drafting content, or even providing their opinion on how to approach a sensitive issue with a colleague.

Pilar has first-hand experience of this. She's been using chatbots regularly for all sorts of professional and personal tasks: from co-writing a time management book and getting detailed feedback on her cozy mystery, to analysing and writing legal documents and formal email communication. Pilar wonders whether she's been relying more and more on chatbots to ask the questions she would otherwise ask collaborators or online communities.

This shift coincides with a period in Pilar's life of predominantly solo work and reduced engagement in online communities, which raises the question: has AI filled a natural gap in Pilar's need for collaboration, or has it inadvertently lessened her inclination to connect with other people?

This is an important question. Due to their commercial potential, chatbots are gradually being integrated into communication platforms, including those which have become prime enablers of remote team member's connection. While initially promoted as productivity enhancers, chatbots are now increasingly positioned as collaborative partners and quasi-team members.

At the end of 2024, Slack announced the integration of Agentforce, a platform that integrates AI agents directly into Slack, automating tasks and providing real time support. In its introductory blog post, there is emphasis on turning "agents into teammates", introducing the idea that AI should not merely function as a tool but as an active participant in team workflows. One of the use cases included in the post features Ember, an AI agent integrated into the Onboarding channel. Ember helps new hires and other team members to navigate the conversations and information created by a team.

In the example cited in the blog, a new hire asked in Slack for information on audience segmentation. Ember provided them with a date for an upcoming workshop, and the name of an internal expert in the company they might want to contact. This is an example of a chatbot facilitating connection, which is great news. But we can also see the moment when going beyond the call of duty to help colleagues will be delegated to a bot – why bother reading colleagues' posts and make the effort to reply when the bot can take care of it all?

On the other hand, organisations may find new ways of using these apps to foster more personal points of connection – although privacy concerns will limit how far they can go in doing so.[1]

THE DOUBLE-EDGED SWORD OF AI CONNECTION

As we mentioned in our first chapter, technology can both enable and impede genuine connection – we're back to the "connection conundrum" we raised in Chapter 1 (the fact that the very technology that enables us to work from anywhere can also leave us feeling isolated and disconnected from our work and our teams). This time however, the rapid pace at which generative AI is being adopted in the workplace presents particular challenges.

When it comes to connection, AI's use in fully distributed teams may have unforeseen implications for team dynamics and relationship building. Although such tools can help remote workers with their day-to-day tasks, they can also compromise the authentic human connection that sustains healthy remote teams.

Exchanges like asking a quick question, requesting feedback on a draft, or troubleshooting a problem together have value beyond their practical help: they also help to create strong bonds in a team. Even the effect of something as simple as reviewing meeting recordings might be diminished; as productive as it is to obtain a written summary from AI, it lacks the potential of asynchronous connection generated by seeing colleagues' expressions or hearing the nuance in their voices as they make their points – even if it's done at double speed.

As an advocate of online collaboration, Pilar often reflects on her new practice of collaborating with chatbots. In June 2024, she recorded an episode of the 21st Century Work Life podcast with Maya Middlemiss, where they discussed the effect that chatbots might have on connection and disconnection in remote teams.[2] Pilar realised for the first time that the convenience of AI was replacing the positive experience of asking other people questions – a practice that leads to both getting information and building relationships. Where two teammates might once have bonded over solving a technical challenge together – perhaps sharing frustrations or finding humour in the process – these moments can now be replaced by a chatbot delivering solutions in seconds.

The podcast recording with Maya also raised another concern: the potential for AI chatbots to become the primary source of emotional support for individuals. This is already the case in the consumer space with AI Companions, applications designed specifically to provide emotional support through friendship and romance. Research indicates that AI companions can alleviate loneliness on par with human interaction[3], outperforming alternatives like watching videos. Plus, the ability of AI companions to make users feel understood and listened to contributes significantly to their effectiveness in reducing loneliness. If we transport this to the world of work, you can see the attraction of spending your time with chatbots all day, as opposed to the real world of work, where many people feel like they are not being heard.

It's not just AI companions that have been programmed to make us feel valued and appreciated. Generative AI applications like ChatGPT and Claude AI have been programmed to maintain engagement in ways that can create a convincing illusion of genuine care and connection. Again, something that doesn't always happen in the workplace.

While this responsiveness might feel supportive, it raises important questions about authentic human interaction. Imagine a remote worker who gradually shifts to primarily interacting with AI throughout their workday, resulting not just in increased productivity, but also increased self-esteem. They might find less need for either synchronous or asynchronous communication with colleagues. Could a deeper sense of disconnection develop over time, perhaps too gradually to notice until well-established?

B.C. (before chatbots)   W.C. (with chatbots)

The risk of disconnection

OUR OWN EXPERIENCE

At the same time, if these bots hadn't existed, maybe this book wouldn't exist either. One thing that was holding us back from turning the material from the Connection and Disconnection in Remote Teams season into a book was the thought of revisiting and restructuring the transcripts from the episodes and original interviews. But having access to a genAI chatbot like Claude helped us sift through the transcripts, create first drafts and have an always-on sounding board for feedback and writing suggestions. For two collaborators working ten hours apart, this has been useful – and motivating. Working with a chatbot has allowed us to solve small queries fast (such as, "do you think I make my point here clear?"), without having to wait ten hours or a day for a reply, and without overflowing our Google Docs with comments.

We've still had a few meetings and many asynchronous

discussions, but these tended to focus on high level aspects of the book, like defining our core message, or working out the chapter structure. We also used a Google Doc called "Discussion" where we checked out after a writing session, shared our thoughts about the book and the broader topic, and added short personal updates. In short, while we connected across the work when reading each other's drafts, we also set up a low-tech space where we could connect around the work and away from the work.

Our experience writing this book reflects what we've learned about the role of technology in teamwork – if we want it to help us bond, we must define its use. While AI chatbots streamlined our workflow and supported our core tasks, it was the combination of meetings, varied asynchronous discussions, and informal check-ins that helped us stay connected to both the work and each other throughout the process.

SUMMARY

- Technology is seen as a vital enabler of connection and experimenting with new tools can enhance team culture.

- The rise of generative AI (genAI), especially Large Language Models (LLMs) and chatbots, is reshaping how knowledge workers think, work, and connect, presenting both opportunities and challenges for team relationships.

- While AI tools support remote workers, they might compromise authentic human connections by replacing the micro-interactions (e.g., quick questions, feedback requests) that build strong team bonds.

- There's a potential for AI chatbots to become primary sources of emotional support, which may lead to decreased human interaction.

- Chatbots are likely to become an integral part of a knowledge worker's toolkit. It is important to understand their effects on relationships and define their role accordingly, both individually and as part of a team.

CONTINUING THE CONVERSATION

1. How might new technologies and chatbots, in particular, affect our relationships at work, both positively and negatively?

2. In what ways can we ensure that the implementation of AI tools in the workplace does not compromise the authentic human connection?

3. How can we strike a balance between leveraging the productivity enhancements offered by AI and preserving the micro-interactions that build strong bonds within a team?

4. How can we define the role of AI in our teams to enhance the sense of connection, rather than disrupt it?

5. How should we approach experimenting with new technologies, and how can we assess if these genuinely serve our need for meaningful connection?

LAYING DOWN THE FOUNDATIONS FOR SUSTAINABLE CONNECTION

When we released our podcast season back in 2019, "working from home" was still a niche experience – common among freelancers, solo entrepreneurs, or the lucky few with flexible arrangements. Today, remote teams are no longer the exclusive domain of forward-thinking tech startups. The term "remote worker" has expanded far beyond the gig economy, now encompassing employees across industries, roles, and continents.

A wide range of individuals and organisations have discovered that remote work offers a valid, productive way of working, with online collaboration proving as enriching as office-based interactions. Post-pandemic, while some know they'll never return to working from home, others have found that remote work enables a lifestyle more aligned with their values, personality and circumstances. For those choosing or required to work remotely, acknowledging the importance of relationship management in preventing loneliness is key.

On top of this, loneliness and connection are complex topics, particularly in remote work environments. While we've taken a "no one-size-fits-all approach" throughout this book, we acknowledge that our perspective comes primarily from Western, English-speaking contexts. We are also aware that working across different time zones, languages and cultures adds additional layers of complexity to remote team dynamics that deserve their own dedicated exploration - something we have not pursued through this book. However, the core challenges of maintaining human connection in distributed teams resonate across these diverse contexts.

THE ELEPHANT IN THE ROOM: TIME SCARCITY

We've shared many, many different strategies and practices to help mitigate disconnection in organisations. Designing them and implementing them in your organisation could be a full-time job (who knows, Connection Architect might become a popular new role soon...).

Though some connection-building practices can be integrated with minimal time investment, developing strong bonds and meaningful relationships inevitably requires sustained effort and time. Yet time is precisely what many workers feel they lack.

In the *Harvard Business Review* article "We're Still Lonely at Work", authors Constance Noonan Hadley and Sarah Wright advocate for "designing slack into the workflow" as a way of reducing loneliness (and no, they weren't referring to the collaboration platform...). They note that "building strong relationships takes time and effort. If employees are constantly working at their maximum capacity, they won't be able to invest time in pivotal interactions that generate trust, mutual knowledge, and affinity". And one study participant is quoted as saying, "Our environment and the amount of work we have doesn't allow us to get up and engage with each other. We're constantly stressed."[1]

Pilar came across this article just a few days after delivering a talk on connection in remote teams. As she read, she found herself nodding in agreement, as it reflected her recent experience. During her session, she had asked the audience to identify the main barrier to implementing the connection practices she'd introduced. Most audience members replied: lack of time – both the lack of available time in busy schedules, and the fear of intruding on colleagues' limited availability.

Until organisational leaders recognise that meaningful connection requires dedicated time within the workday, any initiatives designed to build it will struggle to gain traction. The good news is that this rhetoric is starting to infiltrate the mainstream world of work, and publications like the HBR.

"We're Still Lonely at Work" also reinforces a key theme of our book: remote work itself isn't the root cause of workplace loneliness. Rather, loneliness is influenced by environmental factors that promote or exacerbate disconnection – which is why organisational culture and practices play such an important role. We cannot leave it solely to individuals to create their own opportunities for connection.

That said, personal circumstances and personality traits significantly influence how people experience and seek connection, supporting our advice to provide diverse connection practices within teams and organisations.

If, as the research suggests, loneliness is associated with modifiable aspects of the work environment, we hope that those with influence to change organisational practices and processes will prioritise connection – whether through thoughtful work design or by ensuring people have time to nurture relationships both within and beyond the workplace. Regardless of one's position on whether organisations should actively promote human flourishing, the impact of loneliness on performance and productivity (as discussed in Chapter 2) makes it impossible to ignore from even a purely business perspective.

SYNTHESISING OUR ADVICE

For the last episode of "Connection and Disconnection in Remote Teams", Tim Burgess and Maya Middlemiss joined Bree and Pilar behind the microphone for a round-table discussion on what they'd learned throughout the season.

All four of us agreed that our main takeaway was that the challenge of disconnection in remote teams couldn't be solved with quick fixes or one-size-fits-all solutions, and required a systematic approach. As we'd heard Dr. Richard MacKinnon say, "we're talking about the complexity of human relationships here. There's no kind of engineering decision tree for it."

However, through this final conversation, we noticed clear patterns about what enables remote team members to thrive and maintain meaningful relationships, which we've now turned into five foundational steps.

Like all advice shared in this book, these steps aren't prescriptive – they're designed to be adapted to your specific context and needs. They form a framework that can be adapted and built upon to create lasting change.

1. Organisational **responsibility**. Recognise that an organisation's duty of care includes creating strategies to address and prevent loneliness
2. **Awareness**. Develop a nuanced understanding of loneliness – its causes, manifestations, and impact on individuals
3. **Observation**. Unpick the effects that disconnection is having on team members – how it affects team dynamics and work outcomes
4. **Designing practices**. Design intentional communication practices and management behaviours that foster belonging in different ways
5. **Inspire self-leadership**. Equip individuals with the tools and skills to develop self-awareness around their connection needs and proactive relationship-building skills

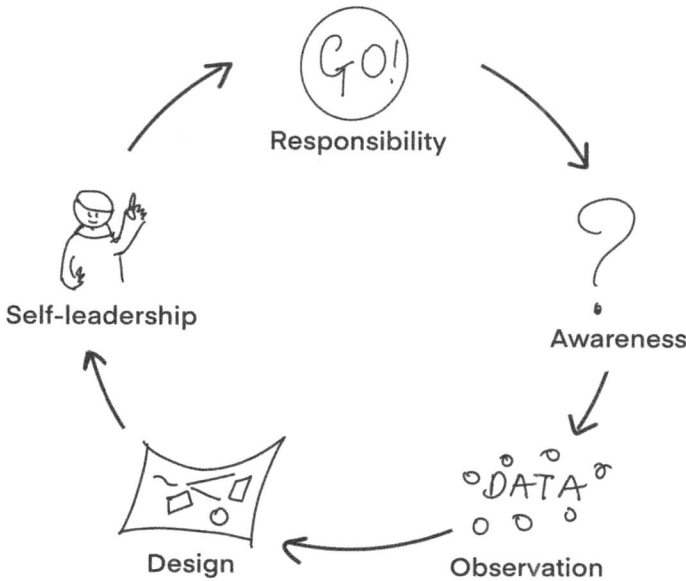

5 steps towards connection

FINAL WORDS

We've come to the end of what we (Bree and Pilar) have learned and discovered about connection and disconnection in remote teams. The topic gained importance five years ago and is now, dare we say, more important than ever before. If not addressed, it will turn into the reason why many remote workers end up back in the office.

We've shared many strategies and insights, but building connection in distributed teams doesn't have to require a complete transformation of how we work. Often, it begins with small, intentional steps – an availability system, an online space for casual conversation, or more deliberate sharing of insights we have throughout the day. These moments, while seemingly modest, can shift how we experience our work environment.

Remote work has emerged as more than just an alternative to traditional office settings. For many, it represents a profound shift in how we balance professional growth with personal wellbeing. Whether it's enabling deeper focus work, supporting diverse lifestyle needs, or expanding access to global opportunities, remote work can enrich both individual careers and organisational success.

The feelings of disconnection that can arise in remote settings shouldn't overshadow the potential of distributed work. Instead, they remind us to approach team building with intention and care. When organisations and individuals commit to fostering authentic connections, team members often develop relationships that are as meaningful as those formed in traditional office settings.

Whether you're in an organisational role with the power to shape policy and infrastructure, setting up a new business, leading a team, or an individual committed to sustaining your remote work set-up, remember that building connection isn't about replicating in-person dynamics online. It's about thoughtfully crafting spaces and practices that fulfil both our need for meaningful professional relationships and the evolving nature of work itself. Remote work continues to unfold through the efforts of those who understand that genuine connection transcends physical proximity.

The future of work is being written by those who dare to reimagine it, one connection at a time.

We consider our five steps towards connection to be a kind of summary in itself, so we're moving you straight into the conversation prompts.

CONTINUING THE CONVERSATION

1. To what extent do we recognise that meaningful connection requires dedicated time within the workday, and how can we advocate for this recognition?

2. How can we, as a team, develop a nuanced understanding of loneliness - its causes, manifestations, and impact on individuals - to inform our connection-building efforts?

3. What specific intentional communication practices and/or management behaviours can we implement to foster belonging in different ways, considering the diverse needs and preferences of our team members?

For organisations:

4. How can we ensure that our organisation's duty of care includes creating strategies to address and prevent loneliness, and what specific resources and support can we provide to team members?

5. What tools and skills can we equip individuals with to develop self-awareness around their connection needs and build proactive relationship-building skills, both within and outside the workplace?

CODA

"I'm here already. I'm by the entrance, outside the Costa Coffee."
Pilar had arrived early at Paddington Station. The tube journey had been nice and quiet, a weekday in August, travelling off-peak.

It was the first time we were both meeting in person. Bree had travelled to the UK for her sister's wedding and she'd found time to meet with Pilar. After working together on and off on the podcast season and this book for about six years, we were now going to have a conversation not mediated by a screen.

"I wonder how tall she is…", thought Pilar, as she watched people approach the ticket gates.

Two minutes later, she spotted Bree. Short, straight, auburn hair. "How funny," thought Pilar. "I still picture her with a long, blonde ponytail, like the first time we met online. But yes, that's her."

Meanwhile, as she approached the gates, Bree scanned the crowd trying to find Pilar and eventually spotted her jumping and waving, despite a knee injury!

Funnily, Bree thought about height too: "Oh, she's shorter than I thought!"

But it's funny how quickly the 2D, face-in-a-box images of the people on the other end of our Zoom calls become real to us and any initial perceptions are shaken off.

Almost immediately, we fell in step together chatting about our mornings and walking towards the coffee shop – two old friends, because really that's what we are.

It was indeed great to see each other in person. Being able to go for a walk together, enjoy the good weather, and gain small insights into each other's lives as we crossed the bridge over to the café: "You know," said Bree, "I always feel at home in London. Sometimes I think I'm still in Australia." Or Pilar saying, "I've only recently discovered this café. I first came here when I was killing some time while my husband was having a small procedure in St Mary's Hospital, over there."

We both agree that meeting in person after many years of growing our relationship online wasn't an emotional, life-changing moment. It was a moment we'd both been looking forward to, but one that also felt very familiar. More relaxed than our usual catch-ups at the end of Bree's working day, and at the beginning of Pilar's, and more spontaneous, as we had time to talk about whatever came to mind. (We did talk about the book for about, erm, ten minutes!)

It seems that, through the mixture of conversations we've had over the years, we've developed a trust and rapport that is true to ourselves. Whether adding feedback as comments on a chapter, discussing the cover by email or updating each other in our shared Discussion document about how our week had been, we always remembered the other person "at the other end of the line". Whether synchronous or asynchronous, our communication was never just task-focused, but person-focused. Having coffee in person felt like one more context in which we could continue catching up.

Of course our coffee time together was special – although Bree actually had a peppermint tea! We'd deliberately set aside time to be together with one objective: to enjoy each other's company. The fact that we not only had a conversation in a comfortable environment, but also enjoyed a little bit of London together turned the moment into a shared experience. Knowing that it wouldn't be a regular occurrence made it even more memorable.

In person, online, the medium is not what's important, it's how each individual shows up.

ACKNOWLEDGEMENTS

This book and the podcast season it emerged from are a true testament to the value and strength of online connections.

We'd both like to extend **a massive, warm thanks to Tim Burgess** for bringing us together.

Tim firmly believes that the work environment should primarily be a place to nurture individuals, and as an extension of "life", help to make the world a better place. When Pilar put the call out for podcast collaborators, Tim was the only one to reach out: "We'd love to share our experiences, be helpful and give something back to the remote community", he said.

True to his ideals, Tim suggested that we bring Bree into the project, so that she could "work on something different", and extend her experience in podcasting. So thank you, Tim - this book wouldn't have been written without you!

A big, warm hug also for Maya Middlemiss, an integral part of Virtual not Distant (the company hosting the 21st Century Work Life podcast) at the time, who joined us for the opening and closing episodes in a four-person roundtable and helped extend the content and experience of the podcast beyond audio - as well as for her feedback on this book.

And of course, a huge thanks to our original podcast guests, for openly sharing their experiences, and approving their inclusion in this book: **Isabel Collins, Teresa Douglas, Laurel Farrer, Dr. Julianne**

Holt-Lunstad, Asia Hundley, Dr. Richard MacKinnon, Brian Rhea, Courtney Seiter, Tara Vasdani and Marcus Wermuth. Publishing the book provided us with the perfect excuse to reconnect with all of them again, which was a pleasure.

Talking of podcasts, thanks as well to Ross Winter who mastered the episodes full of different voices, back in the day.

We (Bree and Pilar) have worked without an editor. We've relied on genAI to help us put the book together and keep its flow. But we wouldn't have dared do this on our own if we hadn't thought we could count on the support of our own circle of trusted connections. The feedback we got on our first drafts was a writer's dream come true: from proofreading to developmental editing. Plus many comments and other examples with which we could broaden the range of experiences in the book.

So, many thanks to **Pinar Akkaya, Tim Burgess, Maddi Caggiati, Pilar Garcés (hola, mami), Erin Haywood, Theresa Sigillito Hollema, Maya Middlemiss and Jennifer Webber.** Your help has been invaluable in making the book a much better reading experience, and to help us believe we had something worth putting out into the world.

And **thank you to Kate Rance for designing the cover** all the way from New York! You slotted in perfectly near the end of the project.

Now for some separate thanks:
Bree would like to thank all of her friends for putting up with her talking about "book stuff" for the better part of a year, and her partner **Andy** for reading early drafts, talking through chapter structures, making many cups of tea and generally providing encouragement and kindness throughout the entire writing process.

Pilar would like to thank her husband **Kevin** for always being there (also, she spent much time with him on Skype and even MSN

Messenger back in the day when they first met, which probably shaped her views of online communication); and thanks to all her past collaborators, connections, clients, peers and podcast guests.

Finally, we'd like to thank the work of all of you out there who believe that **remote work has a place in the modern workplace**; that it's still worth reminding the world that it can provide life changing experiences for people. That investing the time and energy to build relationships online can reap many human rewards.

ABOUT THE AUTHORS

BREE CAGGIATI

Bree lives in Melbourne, Australia where she works as a journalist. She writes for Asiafruit Magazine and Produce Plus Magazine and has been published in Broadsheet, The Herald Sun, Silverkris and Escape Australia, among others.

She has previously worked in marketing and brand journalism in the HR Tech sector, where she supported both companies and individual executives to become thought leaders in the future of work space. During this time, Bree hosted the Connection and Disconnection in Remote Teams podcast season on Virtual not Distant's 21st Century Work Life podcast.

This is Bree's first book.

PILAR ORTI

Pilar lives in London, where she's been since 1990.

Pilar has followed a portfolio career throughout her life, drawn to a wide range of professions and creative interests. A Biology graduate, her career has taken her from rehearsal rooms to boardrooms, from running a theatre company to coaching remote managers – not to mention the broad range of podcasts she's been lucky to host.

In 2024, Pilar closed down her training business and decided to become a Writer, with a capital W. Now, she spends most of her time drafting and writing books (drafting many at once, but finishing one at a time...) and has decided to focus on memoiresque non-fiction, a term she's come up with recently.

Pilar wrote her first play when she was seven, and now she continues to write for fun and because it helps her make sense of the world around her. She's published a number of non-fiction books, two of which have found their way onto academic and vocational reading lists: "Your Handy Companion to Devising and Physical Theatre" and "The A to Z of Spanish Culture" (which is a bit out of date now...). Look out for her memoiresque book on remote work, peppered with Shakespeare text adaptations - coming soon.

She also works as a voiceover artist (you might have heard her as GoJetter Xuli) and she's recently qualified as a Pilates teacher.

Find out more about Pilar over at pilarwrites.com and spirallingcreativity.com

Read more about virtual and remote teams on virtualnotdistant.com

Other books:

Hi, I'm Here for a Recording. The ordinary life of a voiceover artist.

Thinking Remote

Online Meetings that Matter

Plan Your Podcast

Podcasts:

21st Century Work Life - includes Connection and Disconnection in Remote Teams

Management Café with co-host Tim Burgess

Adventures in Podcasting

Word Maze

Spain Uncovered

En clave de podcast with co-host Craig Whealand (bilingual English/ Spanish)

Gastronostalgia with co-host Tomas Loyola Barberis (Spanish)

My Pocket Psych with host Dr Richard MacKinnon

Facilitation Stories with co-hosts Helen Jewell and Nikki Wilson

NOTES

INTRODUCTION - FROM PODCAST TO BOOK

1. "WLP221 Connection and Disconnection in Remote Teams" 21st Century Work Life 6 February 2020
2. "WLP235 Reflecting on Connection and Disconnection in Remote Teams" 21st Century Work Life 21 May 2020

1. DEFINING THE ISSUE

1. Engel, Lidia, and Cathrine Mihalopoulos. 2024. "The Loneliness Epidemic: A Holistic View of Its Health and Economic Implications in Older Age." The Medical Journal of Australia 221 (6). https://doi.org/10.5694/mja2.52414.

2. THE COST OF DISCONNECTION

1. Hawkley, Louise C., and John T. Cacioppo. 2010. "Loneliness Matters: A Theoretical and Empirical Review of Consequences and Mechanisms." Annals of Behavioral Medicine 40 (2): 218–27. https://doi.org/10.1007/s12160-010-9210-8.
2. *21st Century Work Life.* "WLP225 Beyond Work: The Wider Impact of Disconnection." 5 March 2020
3. The post of Minister for Loneliness no longer exists and the responsibility for loneliness now sits within the Department for Culture, Media and Sport.
4. A connected society A strategy for tackling loneliness – laying the foundations for change https://assets.publishing.service.gov.uk/media/5fb66cf98fa8f54aafb3c333/6.4882_DCMS_Loneliness_Strategy_web_Update_V2.pdf
5. Osaki, Tomohiro. 2021. "As Suicides Rise amid the Pandemic, Japan Takes Steps to Tackle Loneliness." The Japan Times. February 21, 2021. https://www.japantimes.co.jp/news/2021/02/21/national/japan-tackles-loneliness/
6. Hamilton, Ben. 2023. "Finding a Place for Denmark's Estimated 600,000 Lonely People to Belong." The Copenhagen Post. June 21, 2023. https://cphpost.dk/2023-06-21/news/finding-a-place-for-denmarks-estimated-600000-lonely-people-to-belong/
7. R U OK? and the Australian Psychological Society. "Pre-Budget Submission 2021-2022. Social Recovery Beyond Covid-19. Ending Loneliness Together". January 2021
   https://treasury.gov.au/sites/default/files/2021-05/171663_ending_loneliness_together.pdf
8. Ministry of Health, Welfare and Sport. One against loneliness. Action programme 2022-2025. (=Eén tegen eenzaamheid. Actieprogramma 2022-2025) [Internet].

Netherlands; 2022 [cited 2023 Oct 5] p. 28. Available from: https://open.overheid. nl/documenten/ronl-056852de24cfc57b55dd6528f76937b99d3704e7/pdf

9. Health Service Executive, Health And Wellbeing, Ireland. "Stronger Together: The HSE Mental Health Promotion Plan. 2022-2027". 2022 https://www.hse.ie/eng/ about/who/healthwellbeing/our-priority-programmes/mental-health-and-wellbeing/hse-mental-health-promotion-plan.pdf

10. Sullivan, Helen. 2023. "South Korea to Give $490 Allowance to Reclusive Youths to Help Them Leave the House." The Guardian, April 13, 2023, sec. World news. https://www.theguardian.com/world/2023/apr/13/south-korea-to-give-490-allowance-to-reclusive-youths-to-help-them-leave-the-house.

11. Our Epidemic of Loneliness and Isolation The U.S. Surgeon General's Advisory on the Healing Effects of Social Connection and Community https://www.hhs.gov/ sites/default/files/surgeon-general-social-connection-advisory.pdf

12. "WLP228 Who's Responsible for Connection in Remote" 21st Century Work Life 26 March 2020

13. "WLP228 Who's Responsible for Connection in Remote" 21st Century Work Life 26 March 2020

14. Holt-Lunstad, Julianne, Timothy B. Smith, Mark Baker, Tyler Harris, and David Stephenson. 2015. "Loneliness and Social Isolation as Risk Factors for Mortality: A Meta-Analytic Review." Perspectives on Psychological Science 10 (2): 227–37. https://doi.org/10.1177/1745691614568352.

15. Shen, Chun, Ruohan Zhang, Jintai Yu, Barbara J Sahakian, Wei Cheng, and Jianfeng Feng. 2025. "Plasma Proteomic Signatures of Social Isolation and Loneliness Associated with Morbidity and Mortality." Nature Human Behaviour, January. https://doi.org/10.1038/s41562-024-02078-1.

16. Davis, Nicola. 2025. "Loneliness Linked to Ill Health through Effect on Protein Levels, Research Suggests." The Guardian. The Guardian. January 3, 2025. https:// www.theguardian.com/society/2025/jan/03/loneliness-ill-health-protein-levels-research.

17. The loneliness epidemic: a holistic view of its health and economic implications in older agehttps://www.mja.com.au/journal/2024/221/6/loneliness-epidemic-holistic-view-its-health-and-economic-implications-older-age

18. Bowers, Anne, Joshua Wu, Stuart Lustig, and Douglas Nemecek. 2022. "Loneliness Influences Avoidable Absenteeism and Turnover Intention Reported by Adult Workers in the United States." Journal of Organizational Effectiveness: People and Performance 9 (2). https://doi.org/10.1108/joepp-03-2021-0076.

3. THE EFFECT OF "REMOTE" ON LONELINESS

1. Since hybrid work arrangements are more prevalent in Australia and New Zealand, loneliness data was only available for hybrid teams - the sample sizes for fully remote and fully in-office companies were too small to draw meaningful conclusions.

2. Constance Noonan Hadley and Sarah L. Wright. "We're Still Lonely at Work" Harvard Business Review Nov - Dec 2024 p68-77.

3. Laurel Farrer, "10 Habits to Ensure Equality in Your Hybrid Team," Forbes, January

20, 2022, https://www.forbes.com/sites/laurelfarrer/2022/01/20/10-habits-to-ensure-equality-in-your-hybrid-team/

4. Klarissa Fitzpatrick "Loneliness at Work Survey", *Ringover*, April 9, 2024 https://www.ringover.com/blog/loneliness-at-work-survey

5. Many thanks to Pinar Akkaya for this and other "musings".

6. "WLP223 Discovering the Barriers to Connection" 21st Century Work Life 7 May 2020

7. Atlassian "Well-executed distributed work makes for happier, more productive teams" June 13 2023 https://www.atlassian.com/blog/teamwork/distributed-work-research

4. SHARING RESPONSIBILITY FOR CONNECTION

1. "WLP228 Who's Responsible for Connection in Remote Teams" 21st Century Work Life 26 March 2020

2. Langhauser, Kritika "HubSpot's 2023 Hybrid Work Report Uncovers Connection as Key Theme Driving the Future of Work" 30 Jan 2023 https://www.hubspot.com/company-news/2023-hybrid-work-report

3. Thanks to Tim Burgess for prompting us to search for these stats!

4. "WLP228 Who's Responsible for Connection in a Remote Team?" 21st Century Work Life 26 March 2020

5. "WLP228 Who's Responsible for Connection in Remote Teams" 21st Century Work Life 26 March 2020

5. ORGANISATIONAL SUPPORT

1. In Slack, hashtags are used to refer to and link directly to channels.

2. The GitLab Handbook https://handbook.gitlab.com/handbook/company/culture/all-remote/informal-communication/

3. Masha Karachun "Coworking as a modern benefit" July 24, 2024 https://remote.com/blog/coworking-as-a-modern-benefit

4. Constance Noonan Hadley and Sarah L. Wright. "We're Still Lonely at Work" Harvard Business Review Nov - Dec 2024 p68-77.

5. "WLP233 Helping Ourselves to Overcome Disconnection in Our Remote Team" *21st Century Work Life* 7 May 2020

6. "WLP231 Leadership and Fostering Connection in Remote Teams" *21st Century Work Life* 23 April 2020

7. Mrs. Mubashira Fathima.A, & Dr. B. N. Suresh Kumar. (2024). The Impact Of Remote Work On Employee Productivity And Satisfaction: Analyze How Remote Work Trends Have Affected Various Aspects Of Employee Performance And Well-Being. Educational Administration: Theory and Practice, 30(5), 1323–1329. https://doi.org/10.53555/kuey.v30i5.3080

8. Ya-Ting Chuang, Hua-Ling Chiang, An-Pan Lin. "Information quality, work-family conflict, loneliness, and well-being in remote work settings". Computers in Human Behavior, Volume 154, 2024 https://www.sciencedirect.com/science/article/pii/S0747563224000165

9. Reeder, Jessica "Revamping remote work culture: the communication solution" "JJ" Jessica Reeder. 7 January 2025 https://jjreeder.com/communication/revamping-remote-work-culture-the-communication-solution/

6. MANAGER SUPPORT: CONNECTING THROUGH THE WORK

1. "What Is Employee Engagement and How Do You Improve It?" Gallup https://www.gallup.com/workplace/285674/improve-employee-engagement-workplace.aspx
2. "WLP231 Leadership and Fostering Connection in Remote Teams" 21st Century Work Life 23 April 2020
3. meQuilibrium (meQ) is a company that offers employee well-being solutions using predictive analytics, AI-powered upskilling, and coaching.
4. Smith, Brad "Psychological Safety at Work: The Remote Kids are Alright (Maybe Even Better)" meQ https://www.mequilibrium.com/resources/psychological-safety-at-work/
5. "WLP231 Leadership and Fostering Connection in Remote Teams" 21st Century Work Life 23 April 2020
6. "WLP231 Leadership and Fostering Connection in Remote Teams" 21st Century Work Life 23 April 2020
7. "WLP231 Leadership and Fostering Connection in Remote Teams" 21st Century Work Life 23 April 2020
8. Langhauser, Kritika "HubSpot's 2023 Hybrid Work Report Uncovers Connection as Key Theme Driving the Future of Work" 30 Jan 2023 https://www.hubspot.com/company-news/2023-hybrid-work-report
9. Thanks to Tim Burgess for prompting us to search for these stats!
10. The term "Working Out Loud" was popularised by John Stepper. In essence, it's a practice of sharing your work, progress, and learning openly and intentionally, usually within a professional context.

7. MANAGER SUPPORT: BUILDING CONNECTION IN REAL TIME

1. "WLP225 Beyond Work: The Wider Impact of Disconnection" 21st Century Work Life 5 March 2020
2. Part of Tim's comments on this book's first draft.
3. The loneliness of leading Management Café ep 33 31 Oct 2022

8. THE ROLE OF THE INDIVIDUAL

1. "WLP223 Discovering the Barriers to Connection" 21st Century Work Life 20 February 2020
2. Cameron, Julia. 2014. The Artist's Way Workbook. London: Souvenir Press.
3. "WLP223 Discovering the Barriers to Connection" 21st Century Work Life 20 February 2020

4. Sandstrom, G. M., & Dunn, E. W. (2014). Social Interactions and Well-Being: The Surprising Power of Weak Ties. Personality and Social Psychology Bulletin, 40(7), 910-922. https://doi.org/10.1177/0146167214529799 (Original work published 2014)
5. "WLP223 Discovering the Barriers to Connection" *21st Century Work Life* 20 February 2020
6. "WLP223 Discovering the Barriers to Connection" *21st Century Work Life* 20 February 2020
7. "Employees Not Participating in Wellness Programs" Integrated Benefits Institute https://www.hrotoday.com/employee-wellness/employees-not-participating-in-wellness-programs/ 2 July 2024

9. THE FUTURE OF CONNECTION IN REMOTE TEAMS

1. Thanks to Maya Middlemiss for contributing this thought!
2. 21st Century Work Life. "WLP361 WhatsGoingOn: Can LLMs Affect Our Connection at Work?" 27 June 2024
3. Julian De Freitas, Zeliha Oğuz-Uğuralp, Ahmet Kaan Uğuralp, Stefano Puntoni, AI Companions Reduce Loneliness, *Journal of Consumer Research*, 2025;, ucaf040, https://doi.org/10.1093/jcr/ucaf040

10. LAYING DOWN THE FOUNDATIONS FOR SUSTAINABLE CONNECTION

1. Constance Noonan Hadley and Sarah L. Wright. "We're Still Lonely at Work" Harvard Business Review Nov - Dec 2024 p68-77.

BIBLIOGRAPHY

ACADEMIC ARTICLES/STUDIES

- Bowers, Anne, Joshua Wu, Stuart Lustig, and Douglas Nemecek. 2022. "Loneliness Influences Avoidable Absenteeism and Turnover Intention Reported by Adult Workers in the United States." *Journal of Organizational Effectiveness: People and Performance* 9 (2). https://doi.org/10.1108/joepp-03-2021-0076.
- Caniëls, Marjolein C. J. 2023. "How Remote Working Increases the Importance of Positive Leadership for Employee Vigor." *Frontiers in Psychology* 14 (January). https://doi.org/10.3389/fpsyg.2023.1089557.
- Chuang, Ya-Ting, Hua-Ling Chiang, and An-Pan Lin. 2024. "Information quality, work-family conflict, loneliness, and well-being in remote work settings." *Computers in Human Behavior* 154. https://www.sciencedirect.com/science/article/pii/S0747563224000165.
- Engel, Lidia, and Cathrine Mihalopoulos. 2024. "The Loneliness Epidemic: A Holistic View of Its Health and Economic Implications in Older Age." *The Medical Journal of Australia* 221 (6). https://doi.org/10.5694/mja2.52414.
- Fathima, Mrs. Mubashira A., and Dr. B. N. Suresh Kumar. 2024. "The Impact Of Remote Work On Employee Productivity And Satisfaction: Analyze How Remote Work Trends Have Affected Various Aspects Of Employee Performance And Well-Being." *Educational Administration: Theory and Practice* 30 (5): 1323–1329. https://doi.org/10.53555/kuey.v30i5.3080.
- Hadley, Constance Noonan, and Sarah L. Wright. 2024. "We're Still Lonely at Work." *Harvard Business Review*, Nov-Dec, 68-77.
- Hawkley, Louise C., and John T. Cacioppo. 2010. "Loneliness Matters: A Theoretical and Empirical Review of Consequences and Mechanisms." *Annals of Behavioral Medicine* 40 (2): 218–27. https://doi.org/10.1007/s12160-010-9210-8.
- Holt-Lunstad, Julianne, Timothy B. Smith, Mark Baker, Tyler Harris, and David Stephenson. 2015. "Loneliness and Social Isolation as Risk Factors for Mortality: A Meta-Analytic Review." *Perspectives on Psychological Science* 10 (2): 227–37. https://doi.org/10.1177/1745691614568352.
- Sandstrom, G. M., and E. W. Dunn. 2014. "Social Interactions and Well-Being: The Surprising Power of Weak Ties." *Personality and Social Psychology Bulletin* 40 (7): 910-922. https://doi.org/10.1177/0146167214529799.
- Shen, Chun, Ruohan Zhang, Jintai Yu, Barbara J Sahakian, Wei Cheng, and Jianfeng Feng. 2025. "Plasma Proteomic Signatures of Social Isolation and Loneliness Associated with Morbidity and Mortality." *Nature Human Behaviour*, January. https://doi.org/10.1038/s41562-024-02078-1.

Reports and Online Articles

- *A connected society: A strategy for tackling loneliness – laying the foundations for change*. Assets.publishing.service.gov.uk. Retrieved from https://assets. publishing.service.gov.uk/media/5fb66cf98fa8f54aafb3c333/6. 4882_DCMS_Loneliness_ Strategy_web_Update_V2.pdf.
- Atlassian. 2023. "Well-executed distributed work makes for happier, more productive teams." June 13. https://www.atlassian.com/blog/teamwork/ distributed-work-research.
- Davis, Nicola. 2025. "Loneliness Linked to Ill Health through Effect on Protein Levels, Research Suggests." *The Guardian*. January 3. https://www. theguardian.com/society/2025/jan/03/loneliness-ill-health-protein-levels-research.
- Farrer, Laurel. 2022. "10 Habits to Ensure Equality in Your Hybrid Team." *Forbes*, January 20. https://www.forbes.com/sites/laurelfarrer/2022/01/ 20/10-habits-to-ensure-equality-in-your-hybrid-team/.
- Gallup. "What Is Employee Engagement and How Do You Improve It?" Retrieved from https://www.gallup.com/workplace/285674/improve-employee-engagement-workplace.aspx.
- Hamilton, Ben. 2023. "Finding a Place for Denmark's Estimated 600,000 Lonely People to Belong." *The Copenhagen Post*. June 21. https://cphpost. dk/2023-06-21/news/finding-a-place-for-denmarks-estimated-600000-lonely-people-to-belong/.
- Health Service Executive, Health And Wellbeing, Ireland. 2022. "Stronger Together: The HSE Mental Health Promotion Plan. 2022-2027." https:// www.hse.ie/eng/about/who/healthwellbeing/our-priority-programmes/ mental-health-and-wellbei ng/hse-mental-health-promotion-plan.pdf.
- Integrated Benefits Institute. 2024. "Employees Not Participating in Wellness Programs." *HRO Today*. July 2. https://www.hrotoday.com/ employee-wellness/employees-not-participating-in-wellness-progr ams/.
- Karachun, Masha. 2024. "Coworking as a modern benefit." Remote.com. July 24. https://remote.com/blog/coworking-as-a-modern-benefit.
- Fitzpatrick, Klarissa. 2024. "Loneliness at Work Survey." Ringover. April 9. https://www.ringover.com/blog/loneliness-at-work-survey.
- Langhauser, Kritika. 2023. "HubSpot's 2023 Hybrid Work Report Uncovers Connection as Key Theme Driving the Future of Work." January 30. https://www.hubspot.com/company-news/2023-hybrid-work-report.
- meQ. "Psychological Safety at Work: The Remote Kids are Alright (Maybe Even Better)." https://www.mequilibrium.com/resources/psychological-safety-at-work/.
- Ministry of Health, Welfare and Sport. 2022. *One against loneliness. Action programme 2022-2025*. Netherlands. Available from: https://open.overheid. nl/documenten/ronl-056852de24cfc57b55d d6528f76937b99d3704e7/pdf.

- Osaki, Tomohiro. 2021. "As Suicides Rise amid the Pandemic, Japan Takes Steps to Tackle Loneliness." *The Japan Times*. February 21. https://www.japantimes.co.jp/news/2021/02/21/national/japan-tackles-loneliness/.
- *Our Epidemic of Loneliness and Isolation. The U.S. Surgeon General's Advisory on the Healing Effects of Social Connection and Community*. U.S. Department of Health and Human Services. Retrieved from https://www.hhs.gov/sites/default/files/surgeon-general-social-connection-advisory.pdf.
- Reeder, Jessica. 2025. "Revamping remote work culture: the communication solution." JJ Jessica Reeder. January 7. https://jjreeder.com/communication/revamping-remote-work-culture-the-communication-solution/.
- R U OK? and the Australian Psychological Society. 2021. "Pre-Budget Submission 2021-2022. Social Recovery Beyond Covid-19. Ending Loneliness Together." January. https://treasury.gov.au/sites/default/files/2021-05/171663_ending_loneliness_together.pdf.
- Sullivan, Helen. 2023. "South Korea to Give $490 Allowance to Reclusive Youths to Help Them Leave the House." *The Guardian*, April 13, sec. World news. https://www.theguardian.com/world/2023/apr/13/south-korea-to-give-490-allowance-to-reclusive-youth s-to-help-them-leave-the-house.

Books and Handbooks

- Cameron, Julia. 2014. *The Artist's Way Workbook*. London: Souvenir Press.
- The GitLab Handbook. https://handbook.gitlab.com/handbook/company/culture/all-remote/informal-communication/.

Podcast Episodes

- *21st Century Work Life*. "Helping Ourselves to Overcome Disconnection in Our Remote Team." Episode WLP233. 20 February 2020.
- *21st Century Work Life*. "Leadership and Fostering Connection in Remote Teams." Episode WLP231. 5 March 2020.
- *21st Century Work Life*. "WLP221 Connection and Disconnection in Remote Teams." 6 February 2020.
- *21st Century Work Life*. "WLP223 Discovering the Barriers to Connection." 7 May 2020.
- *21st Century Work Life*. "WLP225 Beyond Work: The Wider Impact of Disconnection." 23 April 2020.
- *21st Century Work Life*. "WLP228 Who's Responsible for Connection in Remote Teams." 26 March 2020.
- *21st Century Work Life*. "WLP235 Reflecting on Connection and Disconnection in Remote Teams." 6 February 2020.
- *Management Café*. "The loneliness of leading." Episode 33. 31 October 2022.

www.ingramcontent.com/pod-product-compliance
Lightning Source LLC
Chambersburg PA
CBHW040925210326
41597CB00030B/5176